Tom Glazer's

Treasury of Songs
for Children

Arranged for the piano by Stanley Lock and Herbert Haufrecht.
("Hush, Little Baby" and "Rock-a-bye Baby" by Michael Fink)

Tom Glazer's
Treasury of Songs
for Children

(Originally published under the title *Tom Glazer's Treasury of Folk Songs*)

COMPILED BY
TOM GLAZER

ILLUSTRATED BY
JOHN O'BRIEN

DOUBLEDAY
NEW YORK · LONDON · AUCKLAND

Acknowledgments

"Now, Now, Now" by Tom Glazer and Lou Singer, copyright Larry Spier, Inc., New York. "The Happy Wanderer," music by Frederick Moeller, words by Antonia Ridge, copyright 1954 by Bosworth and Co., Ltd., London, for all countries. All rights for the United States and Canada assigned to Sam Fox Publishing Co., Inc. By special permission. "On Top of Spaghetti," by Tom Glazer, copyright 1963, Songs Music, Inc., Scarborough, N.Y. "The Big Rock Candy Mountain," (Children's Version) by Tom Glazer, copyright by Songs Music, Inc., Scarborough, N.Y. "The Little White Duck," words by Walt Barrows, music by Bernard Zaretsky, copyright 1950 by General Music Publishing Co., New York. "Dunderbeck," arranged with new words by Tom Glazer, Songs Music, Inc., New York, copyright 1963. "Uncle Reuben," collected and arranged by Tom Glazer, copyright 1945, Songs Music, Inc., copyright 1949. Excerpts from *Music and Life,* by Thomas Whitney Surette, copyright renewal assigned, 1957, to the E. C. Schirmer Music Company, Boston, and used with their permission.

Copyright © 1964 by Tom Glazer.
Illustrations © 1988 by John O'Brien
Originally published under the title *Tom Glazer's Treasury of Folk Songs.*
Art direction by Diana Klemin
Library of Congress Cataloging in Publication Data
Tom Glazer's treasury of songs for children.
Rev. ed. of: Treasury of folk songs. 1964.
Bibliography: p. 9.
Includes index.
Summary: One hundred thirty-one songs for young
people, with lyrics, piano music, and guitar chords.
Includes nursery songs, folk songs, western songs,
and Christmas songs.
1. Children's songs. 2. Folk-songs, English—United
States. [1. Songs] I. Glazer, Tom. II. Lock,
Stanley. III. Haufrecht, Herbert, 1909–
IV. Treasury of folk songs. V. Title: Treasury of songs
for children.
M1997.T749 1988 86-753397
ISBN 0-385-23693-X

Dedicated to Mimi, John, and Peter Glazer

Introduction

My object is therefore to suggest, first, that the perception of beauty is in the highest sense education; second, that music is especially so, because it is the purest form of beauty; and, third, that music is the only form of beauty by means of which very young children can be educated, because it is the only form accessible to them. (From *Music and Life* by Thomas W. Surette, Houghton Mifflin Co., The Riverside Press, Cambridge, 1917.)

These are the songs of the English-speaking children of North America, for the most part the familiar children's songs of today. They include traditional folk songs, composed songs, and some examples of contemporary children's songs whose great popularity give every indication of lasting. Occasionally, I have included unfamiliar verses of familiar songs, verses which I feel worthy of revival.

The songs have been arranged most tastefully for the piano by Stanley Lock and Herbert Haufrecht, except for "Hush, Little Baby," and "Rock-a-bye Baby," which were arranged by Michael Fink. Simple chord symbols have been provided for guitar or banjo. Those guitarists/banjoists who do not play in the rarer folk-instrument keys like E♭, B♭, etc., can resort to the capo and transpose. The voice range has been kept within bounds most comfortable for children's voices—the medium range— and, in fact, for untrained adult voices. The order is alphabetical, not by category. Piano markings, dynamics, and so forth, have been kept at a bare minimum or at zero; how fast or slow or loud or soft I would leave at the option of the player and not confine him or her to preconceived musical notions. Technical difficulties have also been minimized without, I hope, sacrificing good musical standards.

It is difficult not to succumb to the moving profundity-within-simplicity and sense-within-nonsense which great children's songs possess in one way or another. And it is even more difficult not to be moved by the sight and sound of children singing songs they enjoy, a sight and sound which is surely as close to a heaven on earth as we shall find. Surette says: *American children are musical. American adults are not and the chief reason lies in the wasted opportunities of childhood. If the natural taste of our children for music were properly developed, they would continue to practice it and find pleasure in doing so, and thus would avoid the fatal error of postponing their heaven to another time—the great mistake of life and theology.*

The first time I sang before an audience of children, I noticed immediately an inability on their part to refrain from participating. This was at first somewhat disconcerting, and, being unable to stifle their effervescence, I gave in to it in self-defense. I discovered that if to sing for children is purgatory, to sing for *and* with them is a kind of paradise, complete with noise, colds, character defects, and unpredictable attention spans. Since then, we sing together.

Most authorities agree that the nucleus of interest in and response to music is rhythm first; on the authority of children themselves, this is quite true. Very young babies will often respond with their bodies to rhythmic music, leading their parents mistakenly to interpret such response as an indication of special talent. I have at times been informed confidentially by a doting parent that the "favorite" musical composition of their one-year-old is, for example, the last movement of Beethoven's seventh symphony! While the interpretation of this simple response is exaggerated, it is to the greatest good to provide a musical environment from the earliest age—a truism which, like beneficial tonics, should be repeated regularly.

These, then, are the songs of the children of English-speaking North America. While modern psychology—or just plain parenthood—has taught us that there is a great deal more to children than sweetness and light, it is nonetheless true that these are the songs of health and joy and play—in short, of life at its most positive and persuasive and death-denying—at childhood.

Tom Glazer
Scarborough, N.Y.

Bibliography

The Traditional Games of England, Scotland and Ireland, Lady Alice B. Gomme, London, 1894–98, D. Nutt.

Children's Singing Games, Lady Alice B. Gomme and Cecil Sharp, Novello and Co., London, 1909.

The Gateway to Jewish Song, J. Eisenstein, Behrman's Jewish Book House, New York, 1939.

A New Treasury of Folk Songs, Tom Glazer, Bantam Books, New York, 1961.

Games and Songs of American Children, W. W. Newell, Dover Publications, New York, 1962–63.

The Oxford Dictionary of Nursery Rhymes, Iona and Peter Opie, Oxford University Press, London, 1951–52.

The Lore and Language of School Children, Iona and Peter Opie, Oxford University Press, London, 1959.

Music and Life, Thomas W. Surette, Houghton Mifflin Co., Cambridge, 1917.

A Treasury of American Folklore, B. A. Botkin, Crown Publishers, New York, 1944.

English Folk Songs from the Southern Appalachians, Cecil Sharp, Oxford University Press, London, 1932.

The Oxford Book of Carols, Dearmer, Williams and Shaw, Oxford University Press, London, 1928–50.

The Fireside Book of Folk Songs, M. B. Boni, Simon and Schuster, New York, 1947.

A Treasury of Christmas Songs and Carols, H. W. Simon, Houghton Mifflin Co., Cambridge, 1955.

American Folk Songs for Children, R. C. Seeger, Doubleday and Co., Garden City, N.Y., 1948.

A History of Popular Music in America, Sigmund Spaeth, Random House, New York, 1948.

Read 'Em and Weep, Sigmund Spaeth, Arco Press, New York, 1945.

Our Singing Country, and *American Ballads and Folk Songs,* John and Alan Lomax, Macmillan, New York, 1936 et seq., 1941.

Journal of American Folklore, V. 33, 1920.

Nursery Songs, Arr. Leah Gale, Little Golden Books, New York, 1942 et seq.

Two Bugle Calls, O. W. Norton, Chicago, 1903 (date and place of publication not certain; publisher not given).

Musical Times, London, 1940, Article: "The Adventures of a Tune (Under the Spreading Chestnut Tree)."

Contents

Tom Glazer's

Treasury of Songs
for Children

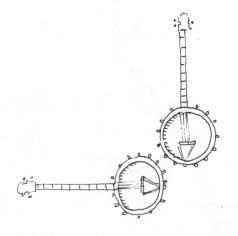

Ach! Du Lieber Augustin

ENGLISH LYRIC: TOM GLAZER

An old song, said to have come from Bavaria, Germany. Hans Christian Andersen referred to it in his fairy tale "The Swineherd." It arrived in England a little later and there it became a popular song called "Buy a Broom."

Oh you love-ly Au-gus-tine, Au-gus-tine, Au-gus-tine,
Ach! Du Lieb-er Au-gus-tin Au-gus-tin, Au-gus-tin,

Oh you love-ly Au-gus-tine, Ev-'ry-thing's gone;
Ach! Du Lieb-er Au-gus-tin, Al-les ist hin;

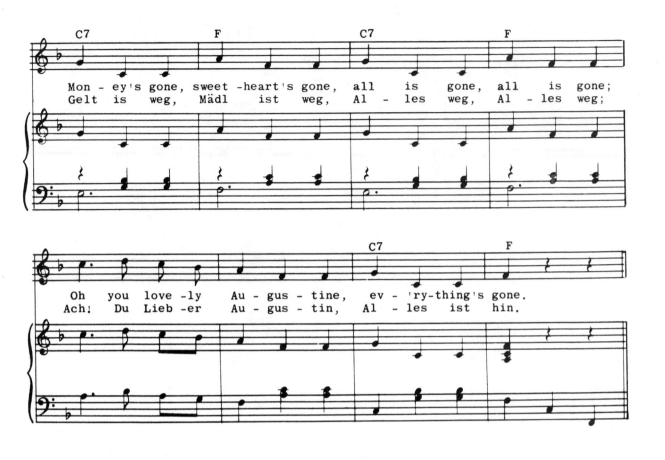

Mon - ey's gone, sweet -heart's gone, all   is   gone, all   is   gone;
Gelt is   weg, Mädl   ist   weg, Al - les   weg, Al - les   weg;

Oh   you   love -ly   Au - gus - tine,   ev - 'ry-thing's gone.
Ach!   Du Lieb -er   Au - gus - tin,   Al - les   ist   hin.

A-Hunting We Will Go

May be related to an old English popular song of the same title by Henry Fielding, of which only the chorus has survived, though changed. In this version it has become a play-party song here and in England.

Oh A - Hunt - ing We Will Go, A - Hunt - ing We Will Go, We'll catch a lit - tle fox, And put him in a box, And then we'll let him go.

America the Beautiful

WORDS: KATHERINE LEE BATES

MUSIC: SAMUEL A. WARD

Miss Bates taught English at Wellesley College for thirty-one years. She wrote many poems, and this one became her most famous effort. There have been several musical settings to these words, including one by her friend and colleague C. G. Hamilton, whose tune the author preferred to this, the one which has overshadowed all others.

O beau - ti - ful for spa - cious skies, For
am - ber waves of grain, ——— For pur - ple moun - tain

ma - jes-ties A - bove the fruit - ed plain! A -

mer - i - ca! A - mer - i - ca! God

shed His grace on thee; And crown thy good with

broth - er - hood From sea to shin - ing sea!

The Animal Fair

An American minstrel song, sung by all the famous old minstrels, including, no doubt, Dan Emmett, the author of "Dixie." The words, "The monk, the monk . . ." are usually repeated **ad infinauseam**.

I went to The An - i - mal Fair, ——— The birds and the beasts were there, —— The big ba-boon, by the light of the moon, was comb -ing his au - burn hair; ——— You

ought to have seen the monk, ——————— He

jumped on the el - e -phant's trunk; —— The el -e -phant sneezed and

fell on his knees And what be -came of the monk? ——

Arkansas Traveler

The "fiddlin'-est" of the country's fiddle tunes. An interesting account of an old-timer's recollection of hearing the tune played often in Salem, Ohio, "before any railroads passed through that country," is given in the Lomaxes' **American Ballads and Folk Songs,** *Macmillan, 1943.*

1. O once up-on a time in Ar - kan-sas, An
2. A trav-el-er was rid - ing by that day, And

old man sat in his lit - tle cab - in door, And
stopped to hear him a - prac - tic-ing a - way; The

fid - dled at a tune that he lik'd to hear, A
cab - in was a - float and his feet were wet, But

jol - ly old tune that he'd play by ear. It was
still the old man did -n't seem to fret. So the

rain - ing hard, but the fid - dler did -n't care, He
stran - ger said: "Now the way it seems to me, You'd

sawed a-way at the pop-u-lar air, Tho' his
bet-ter mend your roof," said he, But the

roof tree leak'd like a wa-ter fall, That
old man said, as he play'd a-way: "I

did-n't seem to bo-ther the man at all.
could-n't mend it now, it's a rain-y day."

3. The traveler replied: "That's all quite true,
But this, I think, is the thing for you to do;
Get busy on a day that is fair and bright,
Then patch the old roof till it's good and tight."
But the old man kept on a-playin' at his reel,
And tapp'd the ground with his leathery heel;
"Get along," said he, "for you give me a pain;
My cabin never leaks when it doesn't rain."

Au Clair de la Lune

The tune is sometimes ascribed to the French composer Lully, and the words to a pastry chef named Crépon, which, if so, would date the song from the time of Louis XIV.

Au Clair De La Lu - ne   Mon a -mi Pier - rot,
In the sil -ver moon - light   Pet -er, my dear friend,

Prê - te moi ta plu - me   Pour é - crire un mot;
Please lend me your pen - cil   just to write a friend;

Ma chan -delle est mor - te, Je n'ai plus de feu;
Can -dle-light is fad - ing, Fire looks pale and odd,

Ou - vre moi ta por - te   Pour l'a - mour de Dieu.
Please don't keep me wait - ing For the love of God.

Auld Lang Syne

Robert Burns's famous words to an old Scottish Lowland tune called "I Feel'd a Lad at Michaelmas." It has become our semiofficial New Year's Eve theme song.

3. We twa ha'e sported i' the burn,
   From morning sun till dine,
   But seas between us braid ha'e roar'd,
   Sin' Auld Lang Syne.
   Sin' Auld Lang Syne, my dear,
   Sin' Auld Lang Syne,
   But seas between us braid ha'e roar'd
   Sin' Auld Lang Syne.

4. And here's a hand, my trusty frien',
   And gie's a hand o' thine;
   We'll tak' a cup o' kindness yet,
   For Auld Lang Syne.
   For Auld Lang Syne, my dear,
   For Auld Lang Syne,
   We'll tak' a cup o' kindness yet,
   For Auld Lang Syne.

Away in a Manger

The authorship of this lovely Christmas song is possibly that of the American James R. Murray, although for many years it had been incorrectly given as the work of Martin Luther. It was known only in the United States. Sometimes the same words are sung to the tune "Flow Gently, Sweet Afton."

1. A - way In A Man -ger, no crib for a bed, The
2. The cat -tle are low -ing, the poor Ba - by wakes, But

lit - tle Lord Je - sus laid down His sweet head; The
lit - tle Lord Je - sus no cry - ing He makes; I

stars in the sky looked down where He lay, The
love Thee, Lord Je - sus! look down from the sky, And

lit - tle Lord Je - sus, A - sleep in the hay.
stay by my cra - dle till morn - ing is nigh.

Baa, Baa, Black Sheep

The bags of wool are said to refer to an export tax placed on this commodity in England in 1275. The tune is the famous French nursery song "Ah, Vous Dirai-je."

Baa, Baa, Black Sheep, have you an - y wool?

Yes, sir, yes, sir, three bags full.

One for my mas - ter and one for my dame, And

one for the lit - tle boy that lives in the lane.

31

Battle Hymn of the Republic

WORDS: JULIA WARD HOWE

The great words were inspired by a visit Julia Ward Howe made to some Union Army camps in 1861, where she heard some soldiers singing "John Brown's Body," the tune of which had come from an old camp-meeting hymn, "Say Brothers, Will You Meet Us?" The Battle Hymn became the most popular marching song of the Civil War with the Northern soldiers.

Mine eyes have seen the glo-ry of the com-ing of the Lord, He is

tram-pling out the vin-tage where the grapes of wrath are stored; He hath

loosed the fate-ful light-ning of His ter- ri- ble swift sword; His

The Bear Went over the Mountain

The famous American play-party song. The same tune is also famous with the very unchildlike lyrics to "We Won't Get Home Until Morning."

Oh, The Bear Went O - ver The Moun - tain, The
Bear Went O - ver The Moun - tain, The Bear Went O - ver The
Moun - tain To see what he could see.
1. To
2. He

see what he could see, To see what he could see,
saw the oth - er side, He saw the oth - er side,

The Bennington Rifles

A fine example of an important song out of a rather unimportant occasion, namely, a skirmish, more than a battle, between some ragged American troops and a detachment of Burgoyne's men on a march down from Canada, during the Revolutionary War.

Why come ye hith-er, in- vad-ers, your mind what mad-ness fills? In our val -ley there is dan -ger and there's dan -ger in our hills; Oh hear ye not the sing -ing of the bu -gle proud and free? Full

2. You ride a goodly steed,
   You may know another master,
   You forward come with speed,
   But you'll learn to break much faster
   When you meet our mountain boys
   And their leader, Johnny Stark;
   They're lads who make but little noise
   And always hit the mark,

   With the rifle (clap, clap), etc.

3. Have you no graves at home
   Across the briny water
   That hither you must come
   Like a bullock to the slaughter?
   If we the job must do,
   Then the sooner 'tis begun;
   If flint and trigger hold but true,
   The quicker 'twill be won,

   With the rifle (clap, clap), etc.

The Big Rock Candy Mountain

(Children's Version)

A special lyric for children written and recorded by me in 1950 or so.

1. On a sum - mer day in the month of May, Oh a
2. There's the ice - cream hill where you have your fill, and the

bunch of kids came lop -ing —— Down a shad - y lane in the
do - nuts grow like flow -ers.—— You can play each day, ev -'ry

sug- ar—cane, For— years they'd been hope, hope, hop-ing; ——— As they
day's a hol i day and the days have a hun -dred' ho -urs. There you

rolled a - long, they — sang a song of a
go to school in a swim - ming pool, and your

land of cake and can-dy, ——— Where a kid can stay when he
fav-'rite cow - boys teach you,——— And you ride a horse, it's your

wants to stay And— ev - 'ry - thing's just dan-dy.———
own, of course, You're so tall that Dad can't reach you.———

CHORUS

Oh, the buzz-ing of the bees In the bub-ble gum trees By the so-da wa-ter foun-tain — At the lem-on-ade springs Where the pop-sick-le sings On The Big Rock Can-dy Moun-tain.

3. You'll have lots of fun, when you hit home runs
Every time you come to bat.
When the doctor's ill, you will feed *him* pills
What do you think of that?
And you'll take a trip in a rocket ship
A hundred miles a minute.
Every day you'll go to the rodeo
And you'll be the hero in it.
Chorus:

Billy Barlow

A Southern song of Old English origin. Hunting was a favorite source of material for songs at a time when it was done more for the necessity of eating than for the luxury of killing.

"Let's go hunt-ing," says Risk - y Rob,

"Let's go hunt-ing," says Rob - in to Bob,

"Let's go hunt-ing," says Dan - 'l to Joe,

"Let's go hunt-ing," says Bill - y Bar - low.

2. "What shall I hunt?" says Risky Rob,
   "What shall I hunt?" says Robin to Bob,
   "What shall I hunt?" says Dan'l to Joe,
   "Hunt for a rat," says Billy Barlow.

3. "How shall I get him?" says Risky Rob,
   "How shall I get him?" says Robin to Bob,
   "How shall I get him?" says Dan'l to Joe,
   "Go borrow a gun," says Billy Barlow.

4. "How shall I haul him?" says Risky Rob,
   "How shall I haul him?" says Robin to Bob,
   "How shall I haul him?" says Dan'l to Joe,
   "Go borrow a cart," says Billy Barlow.

5. "How shall we cut him?" says Risky Rob,
   "How shall we cut him?" says Robin to Bob,
   "How shall we cut him?" says Dan'l to Joe,
   "How shall we cut him?" says Billy Barlow.

6. "I'll take the shoulder," says Risky Rob,
   "I'll take the side," says Robin to Bob,
   "I'll take the hame," says Dan'l to Joe,
   "I'll take the tail bone," says Billy Barlow.

Billy Boy

The earliest versions appeared in the late eighteenth century in England and Scotland. The first lines of the words seem to be related to, or have been mixed up with, the great ballad "Lord Randal." Cecil Sharp, the great British collector of folk songs, found a version in North Carolina in the early 1900s. It became a Hit Parade song here.

Oh where ___ have you been, Bil - ly
Can she bake a cher - ry pie, Bil - ly

Boy, Bil - ly Boy? Oh ___ where ___ have you
Boy, Bil - ly Boy? Can she bake a cher - ry

been, charm - ing Bil - ly? I have
pie, charm - ing Bil - ly? She can

been to seek a wife, She's the
bake a cher - ry pie in the

dar - ling of my life, She's a young thing and
twink-ling of an eye, But she's a young thing and

can - not leave her moth - er.
can - not leave her moth - er.

G   A   D   G   D   A7   D

Bingo

In a nineteenth-century collection of British children's songs, the title is "Little Bingo,"
with additional verses not sung here, about a farmer who loves his ale ("very good
sting-o") and ends, "Now is this not a nice little song?/I think it is, by Jingo!"

The Blue-Tail Fly

(Jimmy Crack Corn)

This has been described as a folk version of a Dan Emmett minstrel song, but since many minstrel songs had folk origins, which came first? It doesn't matter; the song comes last.

When I was young, I used to wait up- on old Mas-ter and pass his plate And fetch the bot-tle when he got dry, And brush a - way The Blue - Tail Fly.

CHORUS (Rhythmically)

Jim-mie Crack Corn, and I don't care, Jim-mie Crack Corn and I don't care,

Jim-mie Crack Corn and I don't care, My Mas-ter's gone a - way.

2. And when he'd ride in the afternoon,
   I'd follow with a hickory broom;
   The pony being very shy,
   Got bitten by a blue-tail fly.
   Chorus:

3. One day he rode around the farm,
   The flies so numerous, they did swarm,
   One chanced to bite him on the thigh,
   The devil take the blue-tail fly.
   Chorus:

4. The pony run, he jump, he pitch,
   He threw old Master in a ditch;
   He died and the jury wondered why
   The verdict was the blue-tail fly.
   Chorus:

5. They laid him under a 'simmon tree,
   His epitaph is there to see;
   "Beneath the earth I'm forced to lie,
   A victim of the blue-tail fly."
   Chorus:

Alternate Verses

2. We went riding one afternoon,
   I followed with a hickory broom,
   The pony being very shy,
   Got bitten by a blue-tail fly.
   Chorus:

3. The pony he did rear and pitch,
   He threw old Master in a ditch;
   The jury asked the reason why,
   The verdict was the blue-tail fly.
   Chorus:

4. So we laid old Master down to rest,
   And on a stone this last request:
   "Beneath the earth I'm forced to lie,
   A victim of the blue-tail fly."
   Chorus:

Buffalo Gals

Pure American, pure joy, pure cornpone.

1. As I was walk-ing down the street,
2. I asked her would she have some talk,

down the street, down the street, A pret-ty lit-tle girl I
have some talk, have some talk, I asked her would she

chanced to meet, oh she was fair to see.
have some talk as she stood close to me.

Buf - fa - lo Gals, won't you come out to - night,

come out to -night, come out to -night, Buf-fa-lo Gals, won't you

come out to -night and dance by the light of the moon.

3. I asked her would she like to dance,
   Like to dance, like to dance,
   I asked her would she like to dance
   As she stood close to me.
   Chorus:

The Bus Song

Of uncertain authorship. First printed, so far as I know, in **Singing and Rhyming,** *Ginn and Co., Boston, 1950, and listed as "Play Song." It is becoming very popular with children in nursery school as a finger-play song and in my concerts, where the children love to act out the words in their seats. I have added some verses: "The baby in the bus" . . . "The bus in the bus . . ."*

1. The peo- ple in the bus go up and down,
   wip - er on the bus goes, "Swish, swish, swish,

up and down, up and down. The
swish, swish, swish, swish, and swish, swish" The

peo - ple in the bus go up and down,
wip - er on the bus goes "Swish, swish, swish"

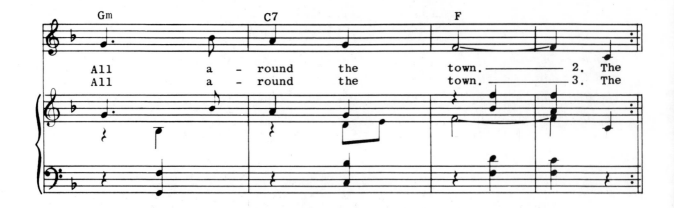

3. The brake on the bus goes, "Roomp, roomp, roomp!" etc.

4. The money in the bus goes, "Clink, clink, clink!" etc.

5. The wheels on the bus go 'round and around, etc.

6. There's a baby in the bus goes, "Wah, wah, wah!" etc.

7. There's a bus on the bus goes, "Bus, bus, bus!" etc.

The Caissons

By Brigadier General Edmund L. Gruber

Was written when General Gruber was a lieutenant in the Fifth Field Artillery in the Philippines in 1908. It was inspired by a hard march the Second Battalion made there in 1907.

O-ver hill, o - ver dale, we have hit the dust-y trail And those
In and out, hear them shout,"Coun-ter-march and right a-bout",And those

Cais-sons Go Roll-ing A - long. Then it's Hi! Hi!

Hee! in the Field Ar-til -ler- y, Sound off your num-bers loud and strong! Wher -e'er you go, you will al - ways know that those cais-sons are roll -ing a - long; Keep them

(shouted)

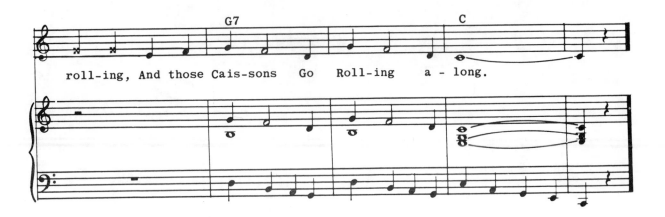

roll-ing, And those Cais-sons Go Roll-ing a - long.

Dust Mops
(Parody Version)

By Peter and Tom Glazer

1. Over hill, over dale, we will dust the dusty trail
    As the dust mops go dusting along;
    Ouch! my head; Ouch! my tail, when we dust the dusty trail
    As the dust mops go dusting along.

CHORUS: So it's sweep, sweep, sweep, we never will weep
         As we are singing this song;
         In dust so deep, we never fall asleep
         As the dust mops go dusting along.

2. Over bed, under sled, we will dust until we're dead
    As the dust mops go dusting along;
    In the chair, in my hair, even in my underwear
    As the dust mops go dusting along.
    Chorus:

3. In the school, dust like fools, underneath the swimming pools
    As the dust mops go dusting along;
    Over land, over sea, who the heck needs gravity
    As the dust mops go dusting along.
    Chorus:

Christmas Is Coming

The custom still exists in this country for panhandlers to say "God bless you," sometimes with unconcealed sarcasm, alas, when they are refused. As did, perhaps, the ancient English beggars at Christmastide in this old song, "If you don't have a ha'penny, then God bless you."

Christ-mas Is Com-ing, the goose is get-ting fat,
Don't have a pen-ny, a ha'-pen-ny will do, If you

Please put a pen-ny in the old man's hat.
don't have a ha'-pen-ny then God bless you, If you

Please put a pen-ny in the old man's hat. If you
don't have a ha'-pen-ny then God bless you.

Clementine

Broke into prominence with college students just after the Civil War.

1. In a cav - ern, in a can - yon, ex - ca -
2. Light she was and like a fair - y, And her

va - ting for a mine, Dwelt a min - er, for - ty -
shoes were num - ber nine, Her - ring box - es with - out

nin - er, And his daugh - ter Clem -en - tine.
top - ses, San -dals were for Clem -en - tine. Oh, my

CHORUS

dar - ling, oh my dar - ling, Oh my

dar - ling Clem - en - tine! Thou art lost and gone for -

ev - er, Dread - ful sor - ry, Clem - en - tine!

3. Drove she ducklings to the water,
   Ev'ry morning just at nine,
   Hit her foot against a splinter,
   Fell into the foaming brine.
   Chorus:

4. Ruby lips above the water,
   Blowing bubbles soft and fine,
   But alas, I was no swimmer,
   So I lost my Clementine.
   Chorus:

5. Then the miner, forty-niner,
   Soon began to peak and pine,
   Thought he oughter jine his daughter,
   Now he's with his Clementine.
   Chorus:

6. In my dreams she still doth haunt me,
   Robed in garments soaked in brine,
   Though in life I used to hug her,
   Now she's dead I draw the line.
   Chorus:

Come, Ye Thankful People, Come

WORDS: HENRY ALFORD

MUSIC: ELVER

Henry Alford wrote the words as a young British vicar in the mid-sixteenth century. Later he became Dean of Canterbury. Elver was organist at St. George's chapel in Windsor; hence, the tune is referred to in hymnals as St. George's, Windsor. It was written for the British Harvest Festival, and therefore became associated with our similar holiday, Thanksgiving.

Come, Ye Thank-ful Peo-ple, Come; Raise the song of

Har-vest-home; All is safe-ly gath-ered in,

Ere the win - ter storms be - gin; God, our Mak - er, doth pro - vide For our wants to be sup - plied; Come to God's own tem - ple, come, Raise the song of Har -vest- home.

2. All the blessings of the field,
   All the stores the garden yield,
   All the fruits in full supply
   Ripened 'neath the summer sky;
   All that spring with bounteous hand
   Scatters o'er the smiling land,
   All that lib'ral autumn pours
   From her rich o'erflowing stores.

Cradle Song

(Sleep, Baby, Sleep)

A very beautiful and ancient German folk song with many variants. Scholars state it is too old to pinpoint its origin.

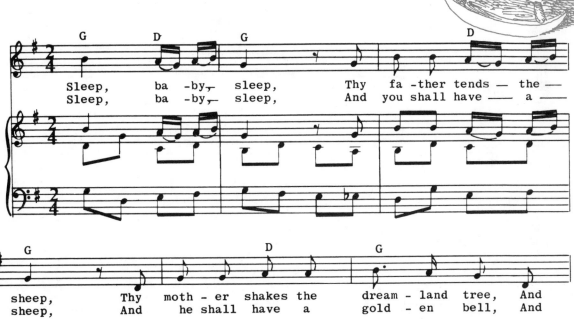

Sleep, ba-by, sleep, Thy fa-ther tends the
Sleep, ba-by, sleep, And you shall have a

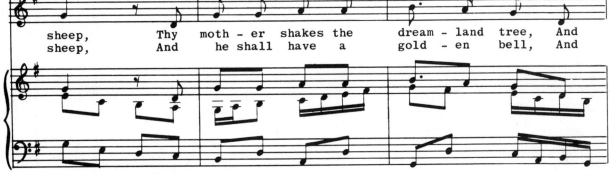

sheep, Thy moth-er shakes the dream-land tree, And
sheep, And he shall have a gold-en bell, And

down come love-ly dreams for thee, Sleep, ba-by, sleep.
play with ba-by in the dell, Sleep, ba-by, sleep.

59

Crawdad

A crawdad is a crustacean, like a lobster, and is found in many a Southern creek. This is one of many, many versions.

1. Sit-tin' on the ice till my feet get cold, hon-ey; Sit-tin' on the ice till my feet get cold, ba-by; Sit-tin' on the ice till my feet get cold,

2. Craw-dad, Craw-dad, you bet-ter dig deep, hon-ey; Craw-dad, Craw-dad, you bet-ter dig deep, ba-by; Craw-dad, Craw-dad, you bet-ter dig deep,

Watch -in' that — Craw - dad in his hole, —— hon - ey,
I'm a - gon -na ramb - le in my sleep, —— hon - ey,

sug - ar ba - by of mine. ——
sug - ar ba - by of mine. ——

3. Sittin' on the ice till my feet get hot, honey;
   Sittin' on the ice till my feet get hot, baby;
   Sittin' on the ice till my feet get hot,
   Watchin' that crawdad rock and trot,
   Honey, sugar baby of mine.

4. Crawdad, crawdad, better go you your hole, honey;
   Crawdad, crawdad, better go you your hole, baby;
   Crawdad, crawdad, better go you your hole,
   If I don't git you, durn my soul,
   Honey, sugar baby of mine.

5. Sittin' on the ice till my feet get numb, honey;
   Sittin' on the ice till my feet get numb, baby;
   Sittin' on the ice till my feet get numb,
   Watchin' that crawdad go and come,
   Honey, sugar baby of mine.

Deck the Halls

Of Welsh origin and uncertain age, although it is old enough for Mozart to have used the tune in a violin and piano duet.

1. Deck The Halls with boughs of hol-ly,
2. See the blaz-ing yule be-fore us,

Fa la la la la la la la la. 'Tis the sea-son
Strike the harp, and

to be jol-ly, Fa la la la la la la la la.
join the cho-rus,

Don we now our gay ap - par - el,
Fol - low me in mer - ry meas - ure,

Fa la la la la la la la la la.
Troll the an - cient
While I tell of

Yule - tide — car - ol,
Christ - mas — treas - ure,

Fa la la la la la la la la.

3. Fast away the old year passes,
   Fa la la la la la la la la.
   Hail the new! ye lads and lasses;
   Fa la la la la la la la la.
   Sing we joyous all together,
   Fa la la la la la la la la.
   Heedless of the wind and weather,
   Fa la la la la la la la la.

Did You Ever See a Lassie?

An American play-party song. It does not appear in Mother Goose collections or in collections of English nursery rhymes; yet, the word "lassie" seems to imply a Scottish origin. The tune is the same as "Ach! Du Lieber Augustin."

Did You Ev-er See A Las-sie, a las-sie, a
lad-die, a lad-die, a

las-sie, Did You Ev-er See A Las-sie
lad-die, Did You Ev-er See A lad-die go

this way and that? Go this way and

that way and this way and that way; Did You

Ev - er See A

Las - sie
lad - die go this way and that?

Dinga Dinga Doodle

A very charming, though obscure, song which deserves wider popularity.

Did you ev - er see a cow in the sky?
Did you ev - er see the sun at — night?

I nev - er did, and neith -er did I. How can a cow stay
I nev - er did, Of course,— you're right. How can the sun —

up in the sky with - out an - y wings with which to fly?
shine at — night when day be - gins when it gives light?

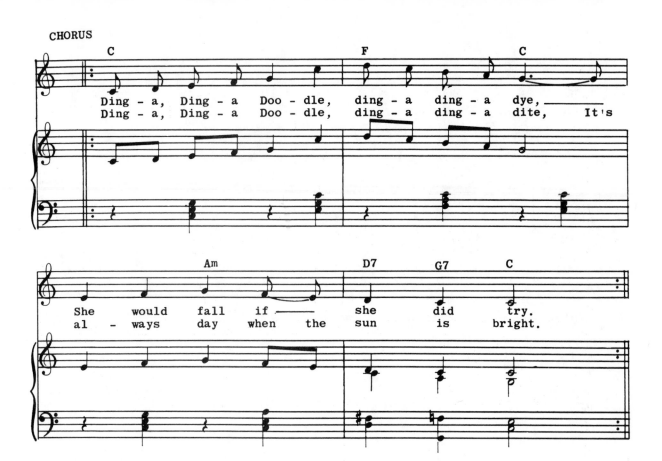

Ding - a, Ding - a Doo - dle, ding - a ding - a dye, _____ It's
Ding - a, Ding - a Doo - dle, ding - a ding - a dite, It's

She would fall if _____ she did try.
al - ways day when the sun is bright.

3. Did you ever see a rose in the snow?
   I never did. The answer is no.
   How can a rose bloom in the snow
   When it's too cold for it to grow?

   Dinga dinga doodle, dinga dinga dow,
   A rosebush sleeps when the cold winds blow.

4. Did you ever see a little boy cry?
   Yes, I did. And so did I.
   It seems such a shame for a boy to cry
   When he could laugh if he did try.

   Dinga dinga doodle, dinga dinga dye,
   It's better to laugh than it is to cry.

Dixie

By Daniel Emmett

Emmett was the famous minstrel man. Although he was born in the North and was a Union sympathizer, his song became very popular as a marching song with Southern soldiers, which upset him very much. It was written for one of his minstrel shows.

I — wish I was — in de land ob cot — ton,
In — Dix - ie Land — whar I was born in,

Old times dar am not for-got -ten, Look a - way! Look a -
Ear -ly on one frost- y morn-in', Look a - way! Look a -

way,   Look   a - way!   Dix - ie   Land.
way!   Look   a - way!   Dix - ie   Land.

CHORUS

Den I wish I was in Dix- ie, Hoo - ray!   Hoo - ray!   In

Dix - ie Land I'll take my stand, To live and die in Dix-ie; A-
way, a - way, a - way down south in Dix-ie, A-
way, a - way, a - way down south in Dix - ie.

2. Dar's buckwheat cakes and Injun batter,
Makes you fat or a little fatter,
Look away! Look away! Look away! Dixie Land.
Den hoe it down and scratch your grabble,
To Dixie Land I'm bound to trabble,
Look away! Look away! Look away! Dixie Land.
Chorus:

70

Donkey Riding

(Riding on a Donkey)

A Canadian merchant marine song. The "donkey" is a crane on board ship.

1. Were you ev - er —— in Que - bec,
2. Were you ev - er in Car - diff Bay,

Stow - ing tim - ber on the deck, Where I al - most
Where the folks all shout, "Hoo-ray! Here comes John with his

broke my neck, Rid - ing on a don - key?
three months pay, Rid - ing on a don - key?"

CHORUS

Hey, ho! A-way we go, Don-key Rid-ing, Don-key Rid-ing;

Hey — ho! A-way we go, Rid-ing on a don-key!

3. Were you ever off the Horn,
   Where the days are nice and warm;
   Seen the lion and the unicorn
   Riding on a donkey?
   Chorus:

4. Were you ever in London town
   Where the bridge is falling down;.
   Seen the King with his golden crown
   Riding on a donkey?
   Chorus:

Down by the Station

So many children's songs become popular hits with adults, as this one did, that they are eloquent musical reminders that the child in all of us never really dies. This is both good and bad, no doubt, but it is hard to find anything bad in the popularity of such a charming song.

(1) F / C / F / C7
Down By The Sta - tion ear - ly in the morn - ing,

(2) F / C7 / F
See the lit - tle puf-fer bel -lies all in a row.

(3) / C7 / F / C
See the en -gine driv - er pull the lit - tle throt - tle,

(4) F / Am / B♭ / C7 / F
Chug! Chug! Poof! Poof! Off we go.

Drill Ye Tarriers

It used to be said that the Irishmen who worked on our railroads were called "tarriers" because of their beards, i.e., "terriers," but an Irish friend insists that to compete with the Chinese who were building the transcontinental railroad from the West, they, the Irish, were exhorted not to tarry—not to be "tarriers."

Ev-'ry morn-in' at sev-en o'-clock, there were twen-ty tar-ri-ers a-drill-in on the rock, And the boss comes a-round, and he says, "Keep still! Come down heav-y on the cast i-ron drill;

CHORUS

And Drill, Ye Tar-ri-ers, drill! And Drill, Ye Tar-ri-ers, drill! For it's

work all day for sug- ar in your tay, Down be-hind the rail-way And

Drill, Ye Tar - ri -ers, drill, and blast, and fire!"

2. The new foreman was Jean McCann;
   By gosh, he was a blamed mean man!
   Last week a premature blast went off
   And a mile in the air went big Jim Goff.
   Chorus:

3. When next payday it came around,
   Jim Goff a dollar short was found;
   When he asked what for, came this reply:
   "You were docked for the time you were up in the sky!"
   Chorus:

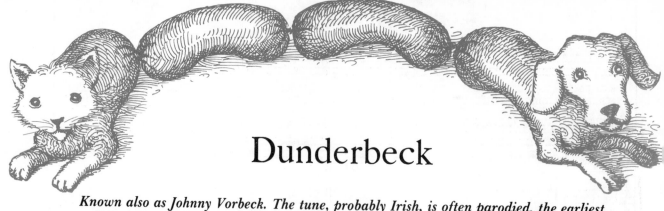

Dunderbeck

Known also as Johnny Vorbeck. The tune, probably Irish, is often parodied, the earliest title in this country being "The Son of a Gambolier," from which came the famous "I'm a Rambling Wreck from Georgia Tech, the Son of an Engineer."

(CHORUS) Oh Dun-der-beck, oh Dun-der-beck, how could you be so
1. (There) was a man from Bri-ar-cliff, his name was Dun-der-

mean? To ev - er have in - vent - ed — the
beck; He sold a lot of sau - sag - es and

sau - sage meat ma - chine? Now all the neigh - bors'
sau - er - kraut, by heck! He made the great - est

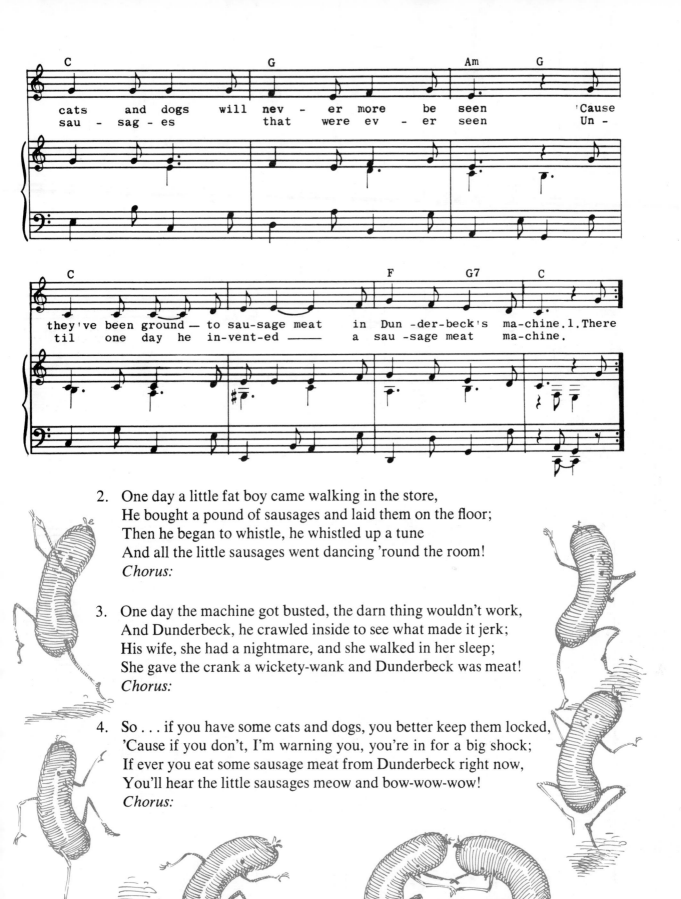

cats and dogs will nev - er more be seen 'Cause
sau - sag - es that were ev - er seen Un -

they've been ground — to sau-sage meat in Dun -der-beck's ma-chine. 1. There
til one day he in-vent-ed _____ a sau -sage meat ma-chine.

2. One day a little fat boy came walking in the store,
   He bought a pound of sausages and laid them on the floor;
   Then he began to whistle, he whistled up a tune
   And all the little sausages went dancing 'round the room!
   Chorus:

3. One day the machine got busted, the darn thing wouldn't work,
   And Dunderbeck, he crawled inside to see what made it jerk;
   His wife, she had a nightmare, and she walked in her sleep;
   She gave the crank a wickety-wank and Dunderbeck was meat!
   Chorus:

4. So . . . if you have some cats and dogs, you better keep them locked,
   'Cause if you don't, I'm warning you, you're in for a big shock;
   If ever you eat some sausage meat from Dunderbeck right now,
   You'll hear the little sausages meow and bow-wow-wow!
   Chorus:

Eency Weency Spider

A Southern song, often used in finger play in the nursery school and kindergarten.

The Een – cy Ween –cy Spi –der went up the wa-ter spout;

Down came the rain —— and washed the spi – der out;

Out came the sun —— and dried up all the rain; Now

Een – cy Ween – cy Spi – der went up the spout a -gain.

The E-ri-e

As is often the case with folk songs, musically and/or lyrically, this lusty, gusty ditty was much more raucous and censorable than now, but it retains its popularity and strength.

1. We were for- ty miles from Al- ban- y, For-
get it I nev- er shall; What a ter- ri- ble storm we
had one night on The E- ri- e Ca- nal.

Oh, The E - ri - e was a -ris -in' And the gin was a - get - tin' low; And I scarce-ly think we'll get a drink till we get to Buf- fa - lo, ——— Till we get to Buf - fa - lo.

2. We were chock up full of barley,
   We were chock up full of rye,
   And the captain he looked down at me
   With his gol-durned wicked eye.
   Chorus:

3. Now the cook was a fine old lady,
   She wore a raggedy dress,
   When the winds blew strong, we hist her up
   As a signal of distress.
   Chorus:

4. The girls are in the Police Gazette,
   The crew is all in jail,
   And I'm the only son of a gun
   That's left to tell the tale.
   Chorus:

Erie Canal
(Got an Old Mule)

The canal, or canawl, as it was often pronounced, opened up the West in 1825. The combination here of the verses in minor key and the chorus in major key is quite rare in American folk songs.

1. I Got An Old Mule and her name is Sal,

Fif -teen years on the E -rie Can - al.
(miles)
She's a good work- er and a

good old pal, Fif-teen years on the E-rie Can-al. We've

hauled some bar-ges in our day, Full of lum-ber,coal and hay,And

we know ev-'ry inch of the way from Al-ban-y to — Buf-fa-lo.

CHORUS

Low bridge, ev-'ry-bod-y down, Low bridge, for we're

com -ing to a town, And you'll al -ways know your work -er, You'll

al -ways know your pal If you've ev-er nav-i-gat- ed on the E-rie Can-al.

2. We better get along on our way, old gal,
   Fifteen miles on the Erie Canal.
   'Cause you bet your life I'd never part with Sal,
   Fifteen miles on the Erie Canal.
   Get up there, mule, here comes a lock,
   We'll make Rome 'bout six o'clock;
   One more trip and back we'll go,
   Right back home to Buffalo.
   Chorus:

The Farmer in the Dell

A Mother Goose song. It was once thought that the original Mother Goose was a Puritan American lady named Elizabeth Foster Vergoose, whose name was discovered in 1665 in an epitaph. But this is probably apocryphal.

The Farm - er In The Dell, The
The farm - er takes a wife, The

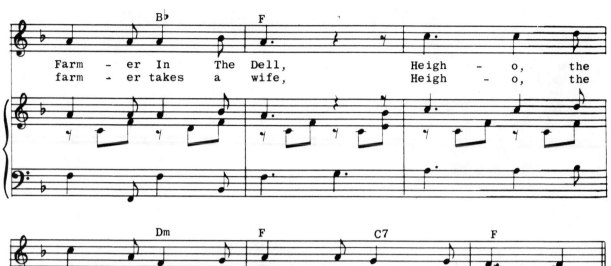

Farm - er In The Dell, Heigh - o, the
farm - er takes a wife, Heigh - o, the

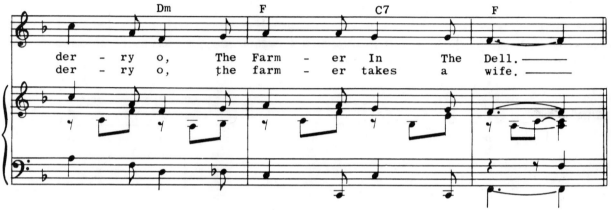

der - ry o, The Farm - er In The Dell.———
der - ry o, the farm - er takes a wife.———

3. The wife takes a nurse, etc.

4. The nurse takes a child, etc.

5. The child takes a dog, etc.

6. The dog takes a cat, etc.

7. The cat takes a rat, etc.

8. The rat takes the cheese, etc.

9. The cheese stands alone, etc.

The First Noel

Was first printed in the 1820s in England, though it was probably much older, and possibly of French origin.

1. The First No-el the an-gels did say, Was to
2. They look ed up and saw a star Shin -ing

cer - tain poor shep -herds in fields as they lay; In
in the East be - yond them far, And

fields where they lay keep -ing their sheep, On a
to the earth it gave great light, And

cold win - ter's night ___ that was ___ so deep.
so it con - tin - ued both day ___ and night. No -

el , ___ No - el , No -el , No - el ,

Born is the King ___ of Is - ra - el.

3. This star drew nigh to the northwest,
   O'er Bethlehem it took its rest.
   And there it did both stop and stay
   Right over the place where Jesus lay.
   Refrain:

4. Then enter'd in those wise men three,
   Full reverently upon their knee,
   And offer'd there in His presence,
   Their gold and myrrh, and frankincense.
   Refrain:

5. Then let us all with one accord
   Sing praise to our heavenly Lord,
   That hath made heaven and earth of nought,
   And with His blood mankind hath bought.
   Refrain:

The Fox

One of our best and best-loved songs. If you like an underdog to win—and who doesn't?—you can derive some satisfaction out of the eternally hunted fox, himself the successful hunter.

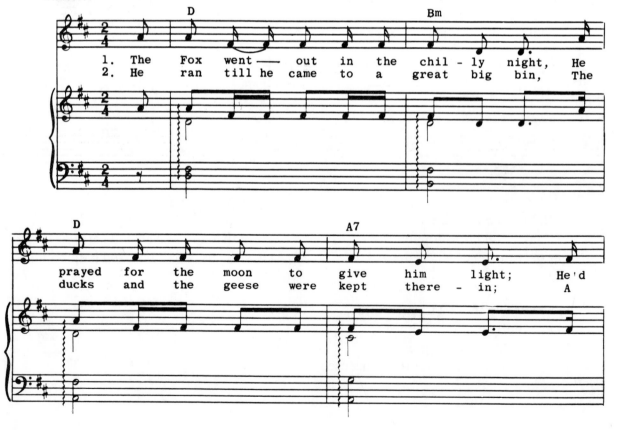

1. The Fox went — out in the chil - ly night, He
2. He ran till he came to a great big bin, The

prayed for the moon to give him light; He'd
ducks and the geese were kept there - in; A

man-y a mile to go that night be-
coup-le of you will grease my chin be-

fore he reached the town - o, town - o, town - o, He'd
fore I leave this town - o, town - o, town - o, A

man - y a mile to go that night be-
coup-le a of you will grease my chin be-

fore he reached the town - o.
fore I leave this

2. He

town - o.

3. So he grabbed a gray goose by the neck
   And threw a duck across his back;
   He didn't mind their "quack, quack, quack"
   And their legs all dangling down-o, down-o, down-o,
   He didn't mind their "quack, quack, quack"
   And their legs all dangling down-o.

4. Then old Mother Flipper-flopper jumped out of bed
   And out of the window she stuck her head;
   Said, "John, John, the gray goose is gone,
   And the fox is in the town-o, town-o, town-o," etc.

5. So John he ran to the top of the hill
   And he blew his horn both loud and shrill;
   The fox he said, "I better flee with my kill
   Or they'll soon be on my trail-o, trail-o, trail-o," etc.

6. He ran till he came to his cozy den
   And there were his little ones, eight, nine, and ten;
   They said, "Daddy, you better go back again
   'Cause it must be a mighty fine town-o, town-o, town-o," etc.

7. So the fox and his wife, without any strife,
   They cut up the goose with a fork and a knife;
   They never had such a supper in their lives
   And the little ones chewed on the bones-o, bones-o, bones-o, etc.

Frère Jacques

A very old French round. During World War II, a parody sprang up in France:
**L'Angleterre, l'Angleterre/Gagnera, gagnera/Gagnera lá guerre, gagnera la
guerre/Contre Hitler, contre Hitler.** *(England will win the war against Hitler.)*

Frè - re Jac-ques, Frè -re Jac - ques, Dor - mez vous,
Are You Sleep-ing, Are You Sleep-ing, Broth-er John,

dor - mez vous? Son - nez les ma - ti - nes,
Broth - er John? Morn -ing bells are ring - ing,

son -nez les ma - ti - nes, Din din don, din din don.
morn -ing bells are ring - ing, Ding ding dong, ding ding dong.

(Repeat ad lib)

The Friendly Beasts

It is not a twelfth-century English carol, as more and more books are declaring, borrowing the same mistake. The tune is an old French carol, "Orientis Partibus," revived by Richard Redhead, the great British hymnist, during the 1850s. The words are by Robert Davis, one-time assistant minister of the Brick Presbyterian Church in New York, who wrote it for a Christmas pageant of Dr. Clarence Dickenson in the early 1900s. Davis died during World War I. It is a monument to a man of God who lived unhappily and died obscurely.

2. "I," said the donkey, shaggy and brown,
   "I carried His mother up hill and down,
   I carried His mother to Bethlehem town.
   I," said the donkey, shaggy and brown.

3. "I," said the cow, all white and red,
   "I gave Him my manger for His bed;
   I gave Him my hay for to rest His head.
   I," said the cow, all white and red.

4. "I," said the sheep with curly horn,
   "I gave Him my wool for His blanket warm.
   I gave Him my coat on Christmas morn.
   I," said the sheep with curly horn.

5. Thus ev'ry beast by some good spell
   In the stable dark was glad to tell
   Of the gift he gave Emmanuel,
   Of the gift he gave Emmanuel.

The Frog Went A-Courtin'

There are many, many versions of this classic, each with its own adherents.

he did ride, With a sword and a pis - tol
Mous - ie's den, Said, "Please, Miss Mous - ie, won't you

by his side, h'm, h'm, h'm, h'm.
let me in, h'm, h'm, h'm, h'm."

3. "First I must ask my Uncle Rat, h'm, h'm, h'm, h'm,
First I must ask my Uncle Rat
And see what he will say to that, h'm, h'm, h'm, h'm."

4. "Miss Mousie, dear, won't you marry me? h'm, h'm, h'm, h'm,
Miss Mousie, dear, won't you marry me,
Way down under the apple tree? h'm, h'm, h'm, h'm."

5. "Where will the wedding supper be? h'm, h'm, h'm, h'm,
Where will the wedding supper be?
Under the same old apple tree, h'm, h'm, h'm, h'm."

6. "What will the wedding supper be? h'm, h'm, h'm, h'm,
What will the wedding supper be?
Hominy grits and a black-eyed pea, h'm, h'm, h'm, h'm."

7. The first come in was a bumble bee, bz-z-z, bz-z-z, bz-z-z, bz-z-z,
The first come in was a bumble bee,
With a big bass fiddle on his knee, bz-z-z, bz-z-z, bz-z-z, bz-z-z.

8. The last come in was a mockingbird, mock, mock, mock, mock.
The last come in was a mockingbird
And said, "This marriage is too absurd, mock, mock, mock, mock."

Get Along, Little Dogies

The best known and most widely sung cowboy song of them all.

1. As I was out walk-ing one morn-ing for pleas-ure, — I spied a cow-punch-er a-rid-ing a-long; — His hat was throwed back and his spurs was a-jing-ling; — As he ap-proached he was sing-ing this song: —

96

Whoop-ee ti - yi-yo, Git A-long, Lit-tle Dog-ies, It's your mis-

for -tune and none of my own; Whoop-ee ti - yi -yo, Git A-long, Lit-tle

Dog -ies, you know that Wy -o -ming will be your new home.

2. Your mother was raised way down in Texas,
   Where the jimson weed and the sandburs grow,
   We'll fill you up on prickly pear and cholla,
   Then throw you on the trail to Idaho.
   Chorus:

3. Early in the spring we round up the dogies,
   We mark 'em and brand 'em and bob off their tails,
   Round up the horses, load up the chuck wagon,
   Then throw the dogies out on the long trail.
   Chorus:

4. Oh, you'll make soup for Uncle Sam's Injuns,
   It's "Beef, heap beef," I hear them cry;
   Git along, git along, git along, little dogies,
   You'll be big steers by and by.
   Chorus:

Go Down, Moses

It was natural for the American slaves to seize on the parallel situation of the people of Israel in bondage to Egypt, to sing so eloquently for freedom.

1. When Is-real was in E-gypt land, Let my peo-ple go; Op-pressed so hard they could not stand, Let my peo-ple go.

CHORUS

Go Down,— Mo-ses,— Way down in E-gypt land,—

Tell — ole — Pha - raoh — to let my peo - ple go.

2. Thus saith the Lord, bold Moses said,
   Let my people go;
   If not, I'll smite your first-born dead,
   Let my people go.
   Chorus:

3. No more shall thy bondage toil,
   Let my people go;
   Let them come out with Egypt's spoil,
   Let my people go.
   Chorus:

4. We need not always weep and mourn,
   Let my people go;
   And wear those slavery's chains forlorn,
   Let my people go.
   Chorus:

5. The devil thought he had us fast,
   Let my people go;
   But we thought we'd break his chains at last,
   Let my people go.
   Chorus:

Go In and Out the Window

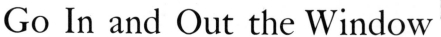

An American play-party song. An earlier variant had the title in plural (windows), with such discarded, I suppose, verses as, "We're marching round the levy (sic . . . levee?)/ For we have gained the day . . . Go forth and choose a lover/For we have gained the day."

Go In And Out The Win - dow, Go

In And Out The Win - dow, Go In And Out The

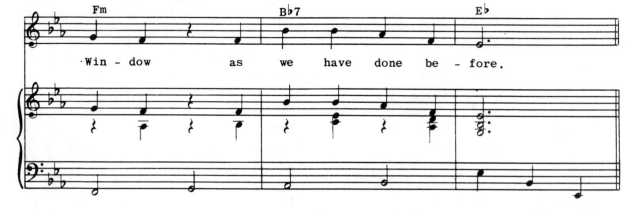

Win - dow as we have done be - fore.

100

Go Tell Aunt Rhody

Sometimes Auntie's name is Nancy, or something else. Nowhere does a song more poignantly express the pathos and hurt of a child when a beloved animal must die.

1. Go Tell Aunt Rho - dy, Go Tell Aunt Rho - dy,
Go Tell Aunt Rho - dy the old gray goose is dead.

2. The one we've been saving, (3 times)
   To make a feather bed.

3. She died on Friday, (3 times)
   With an aching in her head.

4. Old gander's weeping, (3 times)
   Because his wife is dead.

5. Goslings are mourning, (3 times)
   Because their mother's dead.

6. Go tell Aunt Rhody, (3 times)
   The old gray goose is dead.

Go to Sleepy

(All the Pretty Little Horses)

One of those exquisite folk songs with numerous versions, each beautiful. It has been sung by blacks and whites in the days when songs were one of the few bridges between the two races.

Go To Sleep - y, lit-tle ba - by,

When you wake I'll give you some cake;

The Gray Goose

A tall tale of an unconquerable critter.

1. Well,— last Mon-day morn-in', Lawd, Lawd, Lawd, Well,— last Mon-day morn-in', Lawd, Lawd, Lawd.

2. My daddy went a-huntin', Lawd, Lawd, Lawd, (twice)

3. Well, along come a gray goose, Lawd, Lawd, Lawd, etc.

4. Throwed the gun to his shoulder, etc.

5. Well, he pulled on the trigger, etc.

6. He was six weeks a-fallin', etc.

7. He was six weeks a-findin', etc.

8. And we put him on the wagon, etc.

9. And we took him to the farmhouse, etc.

10. He was six weeks a-pickin', etc.

11 And we put him on to parboil, etc.

12. He was six months a-parboil, etc.

13. And we put him on the table, etc.

14. Now the forks couldn't stick him, etc.

15. And the knife couldn't cut him, etc.

16. And we throwed him in the hogpen, etc.

17. And he broke the sow's jawbone, etc.

18. And we took him to the sawmill, etc.

19. And he broke the saw's teeth out, etc.

20. And the last time I seed him, etc.

21. He was flyin' 'cross the ocean, etc.

22. With a long string of goslin's, etc.

23. And he's goin', "Quank, quink-quank," etc.

Green Grow the Rushes-o

A song whose history deserves a book all to itself. It is found in varying ways in many old and new languages, including Hebrew. Its purpose was undoubtedly religious, and it is known sometimes as "The Twelve Apostles."

1. I'll sing you one O! Green Grow The Rush-es O! What is your one O?

One is one and all a-lone and ev-er-more shall be so.

2. I'll sing you two O! Green Grow The Rush -es O! What are your two O?

Two, two the li-ly white boys, cloth-ed all in green— O,

One is one and all a - lone and ev-er-more shall be so.

3. I'll sing you three O! Green Grow The Rush-es O! What are your three O?

Three, three the ri - vals, Two, two the li- ly white boys,

Cloth-ed all in green — O, One is one and all a-lone and ev-er-more shall be so.

4. I'll sing you four O! Green Grow The Rush-es O! What are your four O?

Four for the gos -pel mak - ers, Three, three the ri - vals,

Two, two the li -ly white boys, cloth -ed all in green____ O,

One is one and all a -lone and ev -er -more shall be so.

5. I'll sing you five O! Green Grow The Rush-es O!
6. I'll sing you six O!

5. Five for the sym-bols at your door and four for the gos-pel mak-ers,
6. Six for the six proud walk -ers—

Three, three the ri - vals, Two, two the li - ly white boys,

cloth-ed all in green— O, One is one and all a-lone and ev-er-more shall be so.

Hanukkah Song

Hanukkah, or Chanukah, is the Jewish Festival of Lights, at which a candelabra called a **Menorah** *is lit. The holiday comes at about the same time, more or less, as Christmas, and it is also one of exchanging gifts.* **S'vivonim** *are tops and* **levivot** *(leh-vee-vot) are special pastries. The tune is a Yiddish folk tune; the words are of unknown origin.*

O Ha-nuk-kah, O Ha-nuk-kah, come light the me- no-rah!

Let's have a par - ty, we'll all dance the ho- rah;

Gath - er 'round the ta - ble, we'll give you a treat;

S'vi-vo -nim to play with, le -vi- vot to eat; And while we are

play - ing,   the can - dles are burn - ing__ low;

One for each night, they __ shed a sweet light, to re -

mind us of days long a - go;   One for each night, they __

shed a sweet light, to re - mind us of days long a - go.

The Happy Wanderer

WORDS: ANTONIA RIDGE   MUSIC: FREDERICK MOELLER

A joyous import from Switzerland which made our popular Hit Parade, sung on a recording by a children's chorus.

1. I love to go a-wander-ing, A-long the moun-tain track, And as I go, I love to sing, My knap-sack on my back. Val-de
2. love to wan-der by the stream that danc-es in the sun, So joy-ous-ly it calls to me, "Come! join my hap-py song!" Val-de

113

Hark! The Herald Angels Sing

WORDS: CHARLES WESLEY   MUSIC: FELIX MENDELSSOHN

Wesley, one of the founders of Methodism, and Mendelssohn, the famous composer, never lived to find out that their lyrics and music had been joined by one William Cummings, about 1855.

1. Hark! The Her - ald An - gels Sing —— Glo - ry to the
2. Christ by high - est heav'n a - dored; Christ the ev - er -

new - born King; Peace on earth and mer - cy mild, ——
last - ing Lord; Come, De - sire of na - tions, come, ——

God and sin - ners re - con -ciled! Joy - ful all ye
Fix in us Thy hum - ble home. Veiled in flesh the

na - tions rise; —— Join the tri - umph of the skies; ——
God - head see; —— Hail the In -car - nate De - i - ty, ——

With th' an -gel - ic host pro-claim Christ is — born in Beth-le- hem.
Pleased as Man with man to dwell; Je - sus — our Im-man - u -el!

Hark! The Her - ald An -gels Sing Glo -ry —— to the new-born King.

3. Mild He lays His glory by,
   Born that man may no more die;
   Born to raise the sons of earth,
   Born to give them second birth.
   Ris'n with healing in His wings,
   Light and life to all He brings;
   Hail, the Son of Righteousness!
   Hail, the heav'n-born Prince of Peace!

   Hark! The herald angels sing, etc.

Here We Go Looby Loo

The words "here we go" often introduce children's traditional songs, e.g., "Here we go round the mulberry bush," or, "Here we go round by ring, by ring/As ladies do in Yorkshire . . ." In 1963 a rock-and-roll version of Looby Loo appeared on the Hit Parade.

Here We Go Loo - by Loo, Here We Go Loo - by

light, Here We Go Loo - by Loo

All in a Sat - ur - day night. night.

1.2.3.4. 5.(For Last Verse Only)

I put my right hand in, I put my right hand out; I give my hand a shake, shake, shake and turn my-self a-bout. Oh,

2. I put my left hand in, etc.

3. I put my right foot in, etc.

4. I put my left foot in, etc.

5. I put my whole self in,
   I put my whole self out,
   I give myself a shake, shake, shake
   And turn myself about.

He's Got the Whole World in His Hand

An American spiritual which became famous as the result of a British popular record that came out about 1960.

CHORUS

He's Got The Whole World — in His Hand, He's Got The Whole wide World — in His Hand, He's Got The Whole World — In His Hand, He's Got The Whole World In His Hand. —

1. He's got the little bitty baby in His hand (3 times)
   He's got the whole world in His hand.
   Chorus:

2. He's got you and me in His Hand (3 times)
   He's got the whole world in His hand.
   Chorus:

3. He's got you and me, brother, in His hand (3 times)
   He's got the whole world in His hand.
   Chorus:

4. He's got you and me, sister, in His hand (3 times)
   He's got the whole world in His hand.
   Chorus:

Hey, Ho, Nobody Home

A fine round which very few youngsters fail to run across, if not in lower school, certainly in college.

Hey Ho, No - bod - y Home,

Meat nor drink nor mon - ey have I none,

Yet will I be mer - ry, Hey!

Last Time

Hickory Dickory Dock

The title refers simply to the numbers 8, 9, and 10 in an old English shepherds' dialect used for counting out sheep. In Scotland, in the early nineteenth century, this version has been observed, "Ziccoty, diccoty, doc . . ."

Hick - o - ry, Dick- o - ry, Dock! The

mouse ran up the clock; The clock struck one, and

down he run, Hick - o - ry, Dick - o - ry, Dock!

Home on the Range

*Originally known as "My Western Home" in the 1860s. President Franklin D. Roosevelt
made it into a popular hit in the thirties by declaring it to be his favorite song.*

Oh give me a home, where the buf - fa - lo roam, Where the

deer and the an - te - lope play; ————— Where

seldom is heard a dis-cour - ag - ing word, And the
skies are not cloud - y all day. _____
Home, Home On The Range, _____ Where the

deer and the an - te - lope play; ——————— Where

sel - dom is heard a dis - cour - ag - ing word, And the

skies are not cloud - y all day. ——————

Hot Cross Buns

Originally a street cry, it later became an English nursery play-party song. It is mentioned as a street cry in an English almanac of 1733.

Hot Cross Buns! Hot Cross Buns!

One a pen -ny, two a pen -ny, Hot Cross Buns!

If you have no daugh - ters, If you have no daugh - ters,

If you have no daugh -ters then give them to your sons;

But if you have none of these —— lit -tle elves,

Then —— you must eat —— them —— all your - selves.

D.C.al
FINE

Hush, Little Baby

A beautiful Southern American lullaby.

1. Hush, Lit-tle Ba-by, don't say a word,
2. If that ___ mock-ing bird don't ___ sing,

Ma-ma's gon-na buy you a mock-ing bird.
Ma-ma's gon-na buy you a dia-mond ring.

3. If that diamond ring gets broke,
   Mama's gonna buy you a billy goat.

4. If that billy goat don't pull,
   Mama's gonna buy you a cart 'n' bull.

5. If that cart 'n' bull turn over,
   Mama's gonna buy you a dog named Rover.

6. If that dog named Rover don't bark,
   Mama's gonna buy you a horse 'n' cart.

7. If that horse 'n' cart fall down,
   You'll be the sweetest little baby in town.

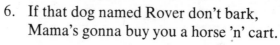

I Had a Little Nut Tree

James O. Halliwell, who published several collections of British nursery rhymes from 1820 to 1860, claimed that the King of Spain's daughter refers to Juana of Castile who came to England in 1506 to visit the court.

I Had A Lit-tle Nut Tree, noth-ing would it bear,
But a sil-ver nut - meg and a gold-en pear; The
King of Spain's— daugh-ter came to vis - it me, And
all— for the sake of my lit - tle nut tree.

I Know a Little Pussy

Most children first hear the major, diatonic scale (do-re-mi) through this song. It does not appear in the great British collections of children's rhymes, songs, and games (Newell, Gomme, Opie), which suggests an American origin.

I Know A Lit-tle Pus-sy, Her coat is sil-ver gray, She lives down in the mead-ow, not ver-y far a-way, Al-tho' she is a pus-sy, She'll nev-er be a cat, For

she's a pus-sy wil-low, Now what do you think of that?

Meow, meow, meow, meow, meow, meow, meow, scat!

I Love Little Pussy

First published in the United States—in Boston, about 1843—in a book called **Only True Mother Goose,** *and in England, about the same time or perhaps earlier, in* **Verses and Hymns for Children.**

I — Love Lit-tle Pus -sy, her coat is so warm, And —
if I don't hurt her, she'll do me no harm. I'll —
sit by the fire —— and give her some food, And —
pus - sy will love me be - cause I am good.

I Ride an Old Paint

The line in this great cowboy song, ". . . to throw the hoolihan . . ." means to throw with a rope, to wrestle a steer or a dogie.

1. I Ride An Old Paint,— I ride an old dam, — I'm goin' to Mon - tan - a to throw the hoo -li -han; You feed them in the cou -lees and wa - ter in the draw; Their

tails are all mat-ted and backs are all raw.

CHORUS

Ride a-round, lit-tle dog-ies, ride a-round — them — slow; For the

Fi-ery and Snuf-fy are rar-in' to go.

2. Old Bill Jones had a daughter and a son;
   His son went to college and the daughter went wrong;
   His wife got killed in a free-for-all fight,
   Still he keeps a-singing from morning till night:
   Chorus:

3. When I die, take my saddle from the wall,
   Put it onto my pony, lead him out of the stall,
   Tie my bones on his back, turn our faces to the West,
   And we'll ride the prairies that we love the best.
   Chorus:

4. I've worked in the town, I've worked on the farm,
   And all I got to show is the muscle in my arm,
   Blisters on my feet and callous on my hand;
   I'm goin' to Montana to throw the hoolihan.
   Chorus:

132

Itiskit, Itaskit

This Anglo-American play-party tune is used in several children's songs in different ways, like "It's Raining, It's Pouring" (which see), "Rain, Rain, Go Away," etc. It is more a chant than a song, consisting mostly of the fifth and the third of the major scale repeated over and over, in descending order. Why these two notes so often are used for this purpose I leave to musicologists to ponder. In England one version was called "Wiskit-A-Wasket."

I-tis-kit, I-tas-kit, A green and yel-low bas-ket, I

wrote a let-ter to my love and on the way I dropped it; I

dropped it, I dropped it, and on the way I dropped it; A

lit-tle boy, he came a-long and put it in his pock-et.

It's Raining, It's Pouring

See "Itiskit, Itasket."

It's Rain - ing, It's Pour - ing, the old man is snor - ing, He went to bed with a cold in his head and he won't get up till morn - ing.

I've Been Working on the Railroad

The exact origin of this famous song isn't known. It could have "just appeared," the way so many folk songs have done, or it could have come from an old-time minstrel show.

I've Been Work-in' On The Rail - road, All the live - long day; I've Been Work-in' On The Rail - road To pass the time a - way.

Don't you hear the whis - tle blow - ing,

Rise up so ear-ly in the morn?

Don't you hear the cap-tain shout-ing, "Di-nah, blow your horn."

Di-nah, won't you blow, Di-nah, won't you blow, Di-nah, won't you blow your

1. horn? ___ 2. horn? Some-one's in the kitch-en with Di-nah,

136

Some-one's in the kitch-en, I know; —— Some-one's in the kitch-en with

Di - nah, strum-ming on the old ban - jo.

Fee - fi fid- dle- e - i - o, Fee - fi fid-dle-e -i - o, ——

Fee - fi fid-dle-e- i - o, Strum-ming on the old ban - jo.

137

Jack and Jill

Several writers have attempted to find very ancient sources for this famous song, as far back as the Norse, or the Middle Ages. Others, by tracing the rhyme "water" and "after," which once did rhyme in English dialect, indicate a source in the earlier seventeenth century.

1. Jack And Jill went up the hill, To fetch a pail of wa - ter; Jack fell down and broke his crown, And Jill came tumb - ling af - ter.

2. Then up Jack got, and home did trot
   As fast as he could caper,
   To old Dame Dob, who patched his nob
   With vinegar and brown paper.

3. Then Jill came in, and she did grin
   To see Jack's paper plaster;
   Her mother whipped her across her knee
   For laughing at Jack's disaster.

Jennie Jenkins

Nonsense songs abound in most folk lores; this one has a most nonsensically surprising line in the chorus, "I'll buy me a fol-de-rol-de . . . etc."

1. Will you wear white, oh my dear, oh my dear?
Will you wear white, Jen-nie Jen-kins? —————— No, I
won't wear white, for the col-or's too bright, I'll
buy me a fol-de-rol-de til-de-tol-de seek a dou-ble

use a cause a roll a find me, Roll,————Jen-nie Jen-kins,

Last time only

roll.————

2. Will you wear green, oh my dear, oh my dear,
   Will you wear green, Jennie Jenkins?
   No, I won't wear green; it ain't fit to be seen,
   I'll buy me, etc.

3. Will you wear blue, oh my dear, oh my dear,
   Will you wear blue, Jennie Jenkins?
   No, I won't wear blue, 'cause blue won't do,
   I'll buy me, etc.

4. Will you wear red, oh my dear, oh my dear,
   Will you wear red, Jennie Jenkins?
   No, I won't wear red; it's the color of my head,
   I'll buy me, etc.

5. Will you wear purple, oh my dear, oh my dear,
   Will you wear purple, Jennie Jenkins?
   No, I won't wear purple; it's the color of a turtle,
   I'll buy me, etc.

140

Jim Along Josie

A play-party song. It's a song in which you suit the action to the words.

Hey Jim A-long,—— Jim A-long Jo-sie,

Hey, Jim A-long,—— Jim A-long Jo, Hey, Jim A-long,——

Jim A-long Jo-sie, Hey Jim A-long,—— Jim a-long Jo.

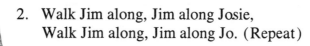

2. Walk Jim along, Jim along Josie,
   Walk Jim along, Jim along Jo. (Repeat)

3. Hop Jim along, Jim along Josie,
   Hop Jim along, Jim along Jo. (Repeat)

(Or anything else you can think of,
like crawl, roll, swing, etc.)

Jingle Bells

BY JOHN PIERPONT

This is really not a Christmas song; it's one for winter in general, for there is no mention of the holiday in it. Over the years, though (the writer died in 1866), it certainly has become one.

Dash-ing thru the snow In a one-horse o-pen sleigh,

O'er the fields we go, laugh-ing all the way;

Bells on bob-tail ring, mak-ing spir-its bright; What

fun it is to ride and sing a sleigh-ing song to-night!

143

John Henry

Our mightiest folk hero, who died competing against the steam drill.

1. When John Hen-ry was a lit-tle ba-by Sit-tin' on — his mam-my's knee, He picked up a ham-mer and a piece of steel, said, "This ham-mer-'ll be the death — of — me, Lord, Lord, This ham-mer-'ll be the death — of —

me."   2.   Well the   man.

2. Well, the Captain said to John Henry,
    "Gonna bring that steam drill 'round.
    Gonna bring that steam drill out on the job,
    Gonna whup that steel on down,
    Gonna whup that steel on down."

3. John Henry said to the Captain,
    "Bring that thirty-pound hammer 'round.
    Thirty-pound hammer with a nine-foot handle
    Gonna beat your steam drill down,
    Gonna beat your steam drill down."

4. John Henry drove about fifteen feet,
    The steam drill drove but nine.
    He drove so hard that he broke his heart;
    And he laid down his hammer and he died,
    And he laid down his hammer and he died.

5. John Henry had a little woman,
    Her name was Mary Ann.
    John Henry took sick and went to bed,
    Mary Ann drove steel like a man,
    Mary Ann drove steel like a man.

6. John Henry said to his shaker,
    "Shaker, why don't you sing?
    I'm throwin' thirty pounds from my hips on down;
    Just listen to the cold steel ring,
    Just listen to the cold steel ring."

7. They took John Henry to the graveyard,
    And they buried him in the sand,
    And ev'ry engine comes a-roarin' by
    Whistled, "There lies a steel-drivin' man,
    There lies a steel-drivin' man."

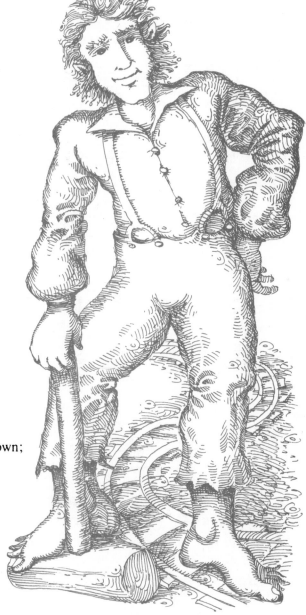

Joshua Fought the Battle of Jericho

". . . and the walls came tumblin' down."

CHORUS

Josh- ua Fought The Bat -tle Of Jer- i - cho,

Jer- i - cho, Jer- i - cho,————— Josh-ua Fought The Bat-tle Of

Jer- i -cho—— And the walls came tum -bling down.

You can talk a-bout your King of Gid-e-on, You can
talk a-bout your man of Saul, There's none like good old

TO CHORUS

Josh-u-a —— at the bat-tle of Jer-i-cho, that morn-ing,

2. Up to the walls of Jericho
   He marched with spear in hand.
   "Go blow them horns," old Joshua cried,
   " 'Cause the battle is in my hand."
   That morning . . .
   Chorus:

3. Then the lamb horns begin to blow,
   Trumpets begin to sound.
   Joshua commanded the children to shout
   And the walls came tumbling down.
   That morning . . .
   Chorus:

The Keeper

In folk song there are very few examples in which the characters are two males. This is the best by far, and is sung in this country much the same way it is in England.

The Keep-er would a-hunt-ing go, And un-der his arm he car-ried a bow,

All for to shoot a mer-ry lit-tle doe a-mong the leaves so — green, O.

(1st Voice)
Jack - ie, boy, Sing you well, Hey down,

Mas -ter
(2nd Voice)
Ver - y well, Ho down,

2. The first doe he shot at, he missed.
   The second doe he trimmed, he kissed.
   The third doe went where nobody wist
   Among the leaves so green, O.
   Chorus:

3. The fourth doe she did cross the plain.
   The Keeper fetched her back again.
   Where it is now it must remain
   Among the leaves so green, O.
   Chorus:

4. The fifth doe she did cross the brook.
   The Keeper fetched it back with his crook.
   Where it is now you must go back and look
   Among the leaves so green, O.
   Chorus:

149

Kookaburra
(Kookelberry)

*An Australian importation, already becoming Americanized from the original title to the
word in parentheses. The title refers to an Australian snake-eating bird with a hoarse cry.*

Koo - ka-bur- ra sits on an old gum tree,____

Mer- ry, mer-ry king of the bush is he; ___ Laugh, Koo- ka-bur -ra,

laugh, Koo- ka -bur - ra, Gay your life must be.

Lavender's Blue

Formerly a love song which trundled into the nursery. **As a love song it appeared as a British broadside ballad between 1670 and 1690. In 1948 it was a popular hit as "The Dilly Dilly Song."**

Lav - en - der's Blue, dil - ly, dil - ly,

Lav - en - der's green. When I am

King, dil -ly, dil-ly, You shall be queen.

Call up your men, dil-ly, dil-ly, Set them to work,

Some to the plow, dil-ly, dil-ly, Some to the cart.

Some to make hay, dilly, dilly,
Some to cut corn,
While you and I, dilly, dilly,
Keep ourselves warm.

Lazy Mary

Some scholars call the song an ancient game. In England a version has a sad ending. Not too much, in short, is known about it.

La - zy Mar - y, will you get up, Will
No, no, moth -er, I won't get up, I

you get up, Will you get up, Oh! La - zy Mar - y, will
won't get up, I won't get up; No, no, Moth-er, I

you get up, Will you get up to - day? ——
won't get up, I won't get up to - day. ——

Little Bitty Baby

(Go, I Will Send Thee)

A citified version of a country-church carol. People insist on calling it "Itty Bitty Baby."
The folk process in contemporary action.

1. Chil-dren, go, I will send thee. How will I send thee?
2. Chil-dren, go, I will send thee. How will I send thee?

I'm a-gon-na send thee — one by one.
I'm a-gon-na send thee — two by two.

1. One's for the Lit-tle Bit-ty Ba - by who's
Two's for — Jo-seph and — Mar - ry

born,   born,   born in Beth -le -hem.

3. Three's for the three old wise men. . . .

4. Four's for the four who stood at the door. . . .

5. Five's for the Hebrew children. . . .

6. Six for the six who had to get fixed. . . .

7. Seven for the seven who went to Heaven. . . .

Little Bo Peep

Although many people have tried to find an older background for Bo Peep, nothing has been discovered past the nineteenth century. But an Elizabethan ballad does contain the rhyme "sheppe" and "boe-pepe."

Lit -tle Bo - Peep has lost her sheep and
Lit -tle Bo - Peep fell fast, a - sleep and

can't tell where — to find them; — Leave them a-lone and
dreamt she heard — them bleat - ing; But when she a - woke, she

they'll — come home, wag-ging their tails — be - hind them.
found it a joke, For they were still — a - fleet - ing.

3. Then up she took her little crook,
Determined for to find them;
She found them indeed, but it made her heart bleed,
For they'd left their tails behind them.

4. It happened one day, as Bo-Peep did stray
Unto a meadow hard by;
There she espied their tails, side by side,
All hung on a tree to dry.

5. She heaved a sigh, and wiped her eye,
And ran o'er hill and dale,
And tried what she could, as a shepherdess should,
To tack each sheep to its tail.

Little Jack Horner

The original Horner, according to a nineteenth-century story, was a steward to the last abbot of Glastonbury in the time of Henry VIII. He was supposed to have pulled out some deeds (plums) from a pie which was being taken to the King.

Lit -tle Jack Hor - ner sat in the cor - ner, Eat - ing a Christ -mas pie; ——— He put in his thumb, and pulled out a plum, And said, "What a good boy am I!" ———

The Little White Duck

WORDS: WALT BARROWS

MUSIC: BERNARD ZARETSKY

A contemporary children's classic.

1. There's a lit-tle white duck sit-ting in the wa-ter, A
lit-tle green frog swim-ming in the wa-ter, A

lit-tle white duck do-ing what he ought - er; He
lit-tle green frog do-ing what he ought - er; He

took a bite of a li - ly pad,
jumped right off of the li - ly pad that The

Flapped his wings and he said, "I'm glad I'm a
lit-tle duck bit and he said, "I'm glad I'm a

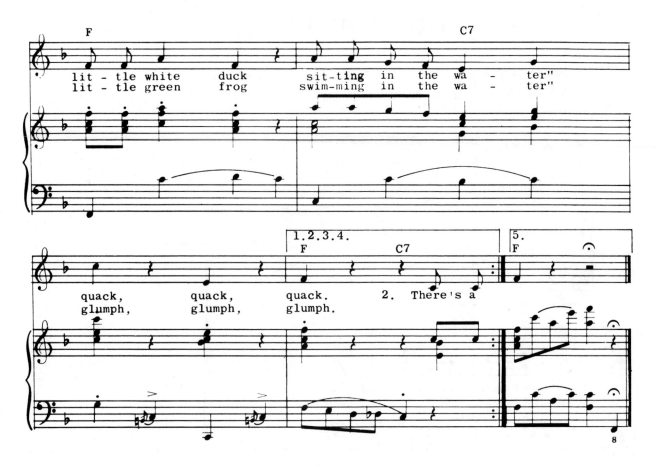

lit – tle white duck sit-ting in the wa – ter"
lit – tle green frog swim-ming in the wa – ter"

1.2.3.4.

quack, quack, quack. 2. There's a
glumph, glumph, glumph.

3. There's a little black bug floating on the water,
   A little black bug doing what he ought-er,
   He tickled the frog on the lily pad
   That the little duck bit and he said, "I'm glad
   I'm a little black bug floating on the water." Chirp, chirp, chirp.

4. There's a little red snake lying in the water,
   A little red snake doing what he ought-er,
   He frightened the duck and the frog so bad
   He ate the little bug and he said, "I'm glad
   I'm a little red snake lying in the water." Sss, sss, sss.

5. Now there's nobody left sitting in the water,
   Nobody left doing what he ought-er,
   There's nothing left but the lily pad,
   The duck and the frog ran away. It's sad
   That there's nobody left sitting in the water. Boo, boo, boo.

London Bridge

A very old English play-party song. It was known first as "London Bridge Is Broken Down." Related play-party games are enjoyed by children in most of the European countries.

Lon - don Bridge is fall-ing down, fall -ing down, fall-ing down,
Build it up with i -ron bars, i - ron bars, i-ron bars,

Lon - don Bridge is fall -ing down, My fair la - dy.
Build it up with i - ron bars, My fair la - dy.

3. Iron bars will bend and break,
   Bend and break, bend and break;
   Iron bars will bend and break,
   My fair lady.

4. Build it up with gold and silver,
   Gold and silver, gold and silver;
   Build it up with gold and silver,
   My fair lady.

The Marines' Hymn

The tune is "Genevieve De Brabant," by Offenbach, of all people. The lyrics are by an unknown marine.

From the halls of Mon - te - zu - ma to the
Our — flag's un - furled to ev - 'ry breeze from —

shores of Tri - po - li   We — fight our coun - try's
dawn to set - ting sun;   We have fought in ev - 'ry

bat - tles in the air, on land and sea; First to
clime and place where— we could take a gun; In the

fight for right and free - dom And to
snow of far - off North - ern land And in

keep our hon-or clean; We are proud to claim the
sun - ny trop -ic scenes, You will find us al - ways

ti -tle of U-nit - ed States Ma - rines.
on the job, The U-nit - ed States Ma - rines.

Mary Had a Little Lamb

The words are among the most famous quatrains in English. And surprisingly, we know the author's name. Sarah J. Hale (1788–1879) wrote them early in 1830 about an occurrence which she said was partly true. They were first published in a magazine she edited called **Juvenile Miscellany.**

Mar - y Had A Lit - tle Lamb,
And ev - 'ry where that Mar - y went,

lit - tle lamb, lit - tle lamb, Mar - y Had A
Mar - y went, Mar - y went, Ev - 'ry where that

Lit - tle Lamb, its fleece was white as snow.
Mar - y went, the lamb was sure to go.

2. He followed her to school one day,
   School one day, school one day;
   He followed her to school one day
   Which was against the rule.

   It made the children laugh and play,
   Laugh and play, laugh and play;
   It made the children laugh and play
   To see a lamb at school.

3. And so the teacher turned him out,
   Turned him out, turned him out;
   And so the teacher turned him out,
   But still he lingered near.

   And waited patiently,
   Patiently, patiently,
   And waited patiently
   Till Mary did appear.

4. "What makes the lamb love Mary so?
   Mary so, Mary so,
   What makes the lamb love Mary so?"
   The eager children cry.

   "Oh, Mary loves the lamb, you know,
   Lamb, you know, lamb, you know.
   Oh, Mary loves the lamb, you know,"
   The teacher did reply.

The Muffin Man

An old English singing-game song, still popular in England and here.

Oh do you know The Muf – fin Man, The
Oh yes, I know The Muf – fin Man, The

Muf – fin Man, The Muf – fin Man, Oh do you know the
Muf – fin Man, The Muf – fin Man, Oh yes, I know the

Muf – fin Man that lives in Dru – ry Lane?
Muf – fin Man that lives in Dru – ry Lane.

The Mulberry Bush

The tune is English eighteenth century. The mulberry bush was traditionally linked to marriage festivals. In 1798, a New York publication entitled it "The Mulberry Tree." The same tune is used for "Here We Go Gathering Nuts in May" with almost identical words.

1. Here we go round The Mul-ber-ry Bush, The
4. This is the way we i-ron our clothes,——

Mul-ber-ry Bush, The Mul-ber-ry Bush, Here we go round The
i-ron our clothes,—— i-ron our clothes, This is the way we

Mul-ber-ry Bush so ear-ly in—the morn-ing.
i-ron our clothes so ear-ly in—the morn-ing.

2. This is the way we scrub our clothes, we
3. This is the way we hang our clothes, we

scrub our clothes, we scrub our clothes, This is the way we
hang our clothes, we hang our clothes, This is the way we

scrub our clothes so ear - ly in —— the morn - ing.
hang our clothes so ear - ly in —— the morn - ing.

Now, Now, Now
(Havah Nagilah)

BY TOM GLAZER AND LOU SINGER

An Israeli folk song which is becoming very well known here. This version was recorded on the RCA-Victor label by the popular singer June Valli.

Come, let's — be hap-py, Come, let's — be hap-py,

Come, let's — be hap-py, Now, Now, Now!

No time — for sor-row, Too late — to-mor-row,

Come, let's — be hap-py, Now, Now, Now!

There is   no time to lose, Put on your danc-ing shoes, Sing a song of

glad-ness, Let the trum-pets blow;   Let's have a lit-tle fling,

Life is   a   pre-cious thing, On your mark, get read-y,   Get   set,

go   Now,   Now,   Now,   Now,   Now,   Now,

Now the song that has-n't been sung, Now the fling that has-n't been flung,

Too man - y hours — wast -ed, Too man - y lips un - tast -ed,

Now is the time, ——— Now is the time ——— The

on- ly time is -Now! on - ly time is Now! ———

Oats, Peas, Beans

Some scholars (the Opies) prefer to see little or no profound significance in old nursery songs. Others (Newell) see many, as he does in this one, going into the meaning of circle dances, and tracing the tune from fourteenth-century French popularity. The mystery stated in the lyric, though, touches us through all generations.

Oats, Peas, Beans And -Bar - ley Grow,

Oats, Peas, Beans And Bar - ley Grow; Can you or I or

an - y - one know How Oats, Peas, Beans And Bar - ley Grow?

Oh, Come All Ye Faithful

(Adeste Fidelis)

May have been written by John F. Wade (Latin words) and John Reading (music), but neither possibility is certain. The English lyric is the result of the efforts of various people.

1. O Come, All Ye Faith - ful, joy - ful and tri - umph - ant, O come ye, O come ____ ye to Beth - le - hem; Come and be -
2. Sing, choirs of an - gels, sing in ex - ul - ta - tion, Sing, all ye cit - i - zens of heav'n ____ a - bove; Glo - ry to

hold Him, born the King of an -gels;
God, —— in —— the —— high - est;
O

come, let us a -dore Him, O come, let us a - dore Him, O

come, let us a - dore Him, —— Christ, —— the Lord.

3. Yea, Lord, we greet Thee, born this happy morning,
   Jesus, to Thee be glory giv'n;
   Word of the Father, now in flesh appearing;
   O come, etc.

Oh, Dear, What Can the Matter Be?

An early version appeared in the 1770s in a book of Scottish songs. The later version, more or less as we know it, became popular in England at the end of the eighteenth century.

Oh! Dear, What Can The Mat-ter Be?

Oh! Dear, What Can The Mat-ter Be? Oh! Dear,

What Can The Mat -ter Be? John-ny's so long at the fair.———— He

prom- ised to bring me a bas - ket of po - sies, A

gar-land of li-lies, a gar-land of ro -ses, He prom-ised to bring me a

bunch of blue rib-bons to tie up my bon -nie brown hair.————

Oh, How Lovely Is the Evening

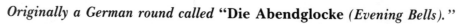

Originally a German round called **"Die Abendglocke** *(Evening Bells)."*

O How Love - ly Is The Ev - 'ning,

Is the ev' - ning, When the bells are

sweet - ly ring - ing, sweet - ly ring - ing.

Ding, dong, ding, dong, ding, dong.

176

Oh, Little Town of Bethlehem

WORDS: PHILLIPS BROOKS   MUSIC: LEWIS REDNER

The words were written by one of the most famous Boston ministers of the 1800s for Holy Trinity Church in Philadelphia about 1868, where the organist wrote the tune.

1. O Lit - tle Town Of Beth - le - hem, How still we — see thee lie; A - bove Thy deep and dream - less sleep the si - lent — stars go by; Yet

2. For Christ is born of Mar - y, And gath - ered — all a - bove, While mor - tals sleep, the an - gels keep their watch of — won - d'ring love; O

3. How silently, how silently,
   The wond'rous gift is given;
   So God imparts to human hearts
   The blessing of His heaven;
   No ear may hear His coming,
   But in this world of sin,
   Where meek souls will receive Him still,
   The dear Christ enters in.

4. O holy Child of Bethlehem,
   Descend to us, we pray,
   Cast out our sins, and enter in,
   Be born in us today;
   We hear the Christmas angels
   The great glad tidings tell;
   O come to us, abide with us,
   Our Lord Emmanuel.

Oh, Susanna

BY STEPHEN FOSTER

This was one of Foster's first successes. It became the theme song of the gold rush in 1849.

I — come from A-la-ba-ma with my ban-jo on my knee, I'm —

going to Lou -'si - an - a, My Su - san - na for to see. It —

rained all day the night I left, The weath -er was so dry, The —

sun so hot I froze my-self, Su - san-na, don't you cry.

Oh, Su - san - na! Oh, don't you cry for me, For I

come from A - la - ba - ma with my ban- jo on my knee.

Old King Cole

The identity of this renowned king has been the subject of lively discussion since the twelfth century. Sir Walter Scott thought him to be the legendary parent of the famous giant Finn McCool.

Old King Cole was a mer-ry old ─ soul, and a

mer-ry old soul was he; He ─ called for his **pipe**, and he

called for his bowl, and he called for his fid -dlers—three.

Ev — 'ry ___ fid - dler ___ had a fid - dle fine ___ and a

ver - y fine ___ fid-dle had he; Twee-dle dum, twee-dle dee, went the

fid - dlers ___ three, twee-dle dum -dee dum-dee-dee -dle dee!

Old MacDonald

It was once called "MacDonald's Farm" in older songbooks.

here a moo,   there a moo,   ev-'ry-where a   moo - moo,
here an oink,   there an oink,   ev-'ry-where an   oink - oink,

Old Mac -Don -ald   had   a   farm,   E - I - E - I - O.

3. And on his farm he had a duck, etc.

   With a quack-quack here and a quack-quack there, etc.

4. And on his farm he had a horse, etc.

   With a neigh-neigh here and a neigh-neigh there, etc.

5. And on his farm he had a donkey,

   With a hee-haw here, etc.

6. And on his farm he had some chickens, etc.

   With a chick-chick here, etc.

(Add your own animals)

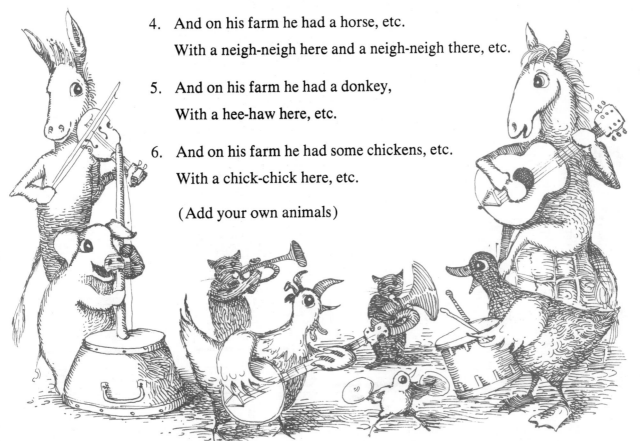

On Top of Spaghetti

BY TOM GLAZER

New words to the famous folk tune "On Top of Old Smoky." Both became popular hits through recordings.

when some - bod - y sneezed.
rolled out of the door.

1.2.3.4.5.
C   (tacet)

2. It rolled off the

6.
C

3. It rolled in the garden and under a bush,
   And then my poor meatball was nothing but mush.

4. The mush was as tasty as tasty could be,
   And early next summer it grew into a tree.

5. The tree was all covered with beautiful moss,
   It grew lovely meatballs and tomato sauce.

6. So if you eat spaghetti, all covered with cheese,
   Hold on to your meatballs and don't ever sneeze.

Pat Works on the Railway

In the 1850s, waves of Irish immigrants came over here, many of them to work as laborers on the railroads. With characteristic Irish wit and eloquence they expressed their feelings about the life in this rousing number.

1. In eight-een hun-dred and for-ty one, I put me cor-du-roy breech-es on, I put me cor-du-roy
2. When we left Ire-land to come here, To spend our lat-ter days in cheer, The boss, he drank some

breech - es on To work up - on the rail - way.
gin - ger beer while work - ing on the rail - way.

CHORUS

Fil- le -me -oo - re-oo - re - ay, Fil- le- me -oo - re-oo - re-ay,

Fil -le - me -oo - re- oo - re-ay To work up- on the rail - way.

3. It's "Pat, do this" and "Pat, do that," without a stocking or a cravat,
And nothing but an old straw hat while working on the railway.

4. And when Pat lays him down to sleep, the wiry bugs around him creep,
Divil a bit can poor Pat sleep while working on the railway.

5. In eighteen hundred and forty-three, 'twas then he met sweet Biddy McGee,
An illy-gant wife she was to see while working on the railway.

6. In eighteen hundred and forty-seven, sweet Biddy McGee she went to heaven,
If she had one child, she had eleven, to work upon the railway.

Pick a Bale of Cotton

A rhythmic work song in which the boast of picking a bale of cotton in one day is only a boast, but singing it makes you feel as if you actually could, and more.

1. Gon-na jump down, turn a-round, Pick A Bale Of Cot-ton, Gon-na

jump down, turn a-round, Pick a bale a day.

CHORUS

Oh Law-dy, Pick A Bale Of Cot-ton, Oh Law-dy,

1.
Pick a bale a day.

2.
Pick a bale a day.

2. Me and my brother, we can pick a bale of cotton,
   Me and my brother, we can pick a bale a day.
   Chorus:

3. Me and my sister, we can pick a bale of cotton,
   Me and my sister, we can pick a bale a day.
   Chorus:

4. I can pick a, pick a, pick a, pick a bale of cotton,
   I can pick a, pick a, pick a, pick a bale a day.
   Chorus:

Polly, Put the Kettle On

When this charming English song, first known as "Jenny's Bawbee (baby)," appeared in 1776, the American colonists were having problems with tea. Some delightful American additions are given below.

Pol - ly, Put The Ket - tle On, Pol - ly, Put The Ket - tle On, Pol - ly, Put The Ket - tle On, we'll all have tea. Su -key, take it off a - gain,

Su - key, take it off a - gain, Su - key, take it

off a - gain, they've all gone a - way.

2. Now put down the ginger cake,
   Now put down the ginger cake,
   Stir the fire and let it bake
   And we'll all take tea.

3. Polly, set the table out,
   Polly, set the table out,
   Move the dishes all about
   And we'll all take tea.

4. Pass around the punkin pie,
   Pass around the punkin pie,
   And the fritters made of rye
   And we'll all take tea.

Pop Goes the Weasel

The tune appears in **Old Nursery Rhymes of France** *and could be French originally. To "pop" means to pawn, and London hatters were wont to pawn the instruments of their trade, known as weasels. This, according to Sigmund Spaeth. It recently became popular (1962–63) through an English recording.*

penny for a spool ___ of thread, A

penny for a nee - dle, That's the way the

mon - ey goes, Pop! Goes The Wea - sel.

Put Your Finger in the Air

By WOODY GUTHRIE

One of several the famous folksinger and songwriter wrote called "Songs To Grow On." It has become one of the most famous finger-play songs in the country.

1. Put Your Fin-ger In The Air, in the air, Put Your
2. Put your fin-ger on your head, on your head, Put your

Fin-ger In The Air, in the air; Put Your
fin-ger on your head, on your head; Put your

Fin-ger In The Air and— leave it a-bout a year, Put Your
fin-ger on your head, tell me is it— green or red, Put your

Fin - ger In The Air, in the air.
fin - ger on your head, on your head.

3. Put your finger on your nose, on your nose, (2)
   Put your finger on your nose
   And let the cold wind blow,
   Put your finger on your nose, on your nose.

4. Put your finger on your shoe, on your shoe, (2)
   . . . . . And leave it a day or two, etc.

5. . . . . . on your chin,
   . . . . . That's where the food slips in, etc.

6. . . . . . on your cheek
   . . . . . And leave it about a week, etc.

7. Put your fingers all together, all together, (2)
   Put your fingers all together
   And we'll clap for better weather,
   Put your fingers all together, all together.

Rock-a-bye Baby

The most famous lullaby in the English language. Many authorities have seen varying significances in the words, one dating them back to the Egyptians. None of these, true or false, explains the enduring popularity of the song. In England it is often "Hush-a-bye Baby . . ."

Rock - a -bye Ba - by, on the tree top,

When the wind blows, the crad - le will rock,

When the bough breaks, the crad - le will fall,

Down will come ba - by, crad - le and all.

Row, Row, Row Your Boat

I heard this parody in Philadelphia as a boy: "Rip, rip, rip your pants/Gently down the seam/Merrily, merrily, merrily, merrily/Hear the ladies scream."

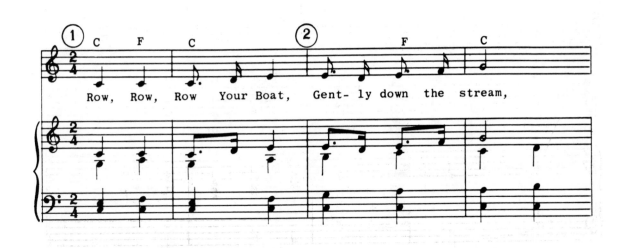

Row, Row, Row Your Boat, Gent- ly down the stream,

She'll Be Coming Round the Mountain

Was once a spiritual, "When The Chariot Comes," changed about by mountain folk. It became very popular in this form with railroad workers of the 1890s.

1. She'll Be Com - in' Round The Moun - tain when she comes,
2. She'll be driv - in' six white hors - es when she comes,

She'll Be Com - in' Round The Moun - tain when she comes,
She'll be driv - in' six white hors - es when she comes,

She'll be
She'll be

G   **G7**

com - in' round the moun - tain, She'll be
driv - in' six white hors - es, She'll be

C   **G**

com - in' round the moun -tain, She'll Be Com - in' Round The
driv -in' six white hors - es, She'll be driv - in' six white

A7   **D7**   **G**

Moun – tain when she comes.
hors – es when she comes.

3. Oh, we'll all go to meet her when she comes,
Oh, we'll all go to meet her when she comes,
Oh, we'll all go to meet her,
Oh, we'll all go to meet her,
Oh, we'll all go to meet her when she comes.

4. We'll be singin' "Hallelujah" when she comes,
We'll be singin' "Hallelujah" when she comes,
We'll be singin' "Hallelujah,"
We'll be singin' "Hallelujah,"
We'll be singin' "Hallelujah" when she comes.

Shoo Fly

A nonsense song of the Civil War, especially well liked and sung by the Negro troops. The line is sometimes included: "For I belong to Company G." And this is an old verse: "I feel, I feel, I feel / That's what my mama said / Like angels pouring 'lasses down / Right down upon my head."

Shoo Fly, don't both-er me, Shoo Fly, don't both-er me!

Shoo Fly, don't both-er me, For I be-long to some-bod-y. I

feel, I feel, I feel like a morn-ing star, I feel, I

feel, I feel like a morn-ing star. Oh feel like a morn-ing star.

The Sidewalks of New York

BY CHARLES LAWLER AND JAMES BLAKE

Written in 1894 and still as famous now as then, and likely to remain so.

East side, West side, All a-round the town, _____ The tots sing "Ring - a - ro - sie, Lon - don Bridge is fall - ing

down." ———— Boys and girls to - geth -er,————

Me and Ma -mie Rorke,———————— We tripped the light fan -

tas -tic On The Side -walks Of New York.————————

Silent Night

WORDS: JOSEPH MOHR   MUSIC: FRANZ GRUBER

Written for Christmas, 1818, in Oberndorf, Austria, by Mohr, the assistant minister, and Gruber, the schoolmaster of the town, who sometimes played the church organ. It is undoubtedly the most beloved carol ever written.

1. Si -lent Night, Ho - ly night! All is calm,
2. Si -lent Night, Ho - ly night! Shep - herds quake

all   is   bright,   Round   yon   Vir   - gin Moth - er   and   Child,
at   the sight!   Glo - ries stream from   heav - en   a - far,

Ho - ly   In - fant   so   ten-der and mild   Sleep   in heav - en - ly
Heav'n - ly   hosts —— sing   Al - le - lu - ia;   Christ the Sav -iour is

peace,   Sleep   in   heav - en - ly   peace.
born!   Christ   the   Sav - iour is   born!

3. Silent Night, Holy night!
Child of Heav'n, O how bright;
Thou didst smile when Thou wast born!
Blessed be that happy morn,
Full of heavenly joy,
Full of heavenly joy!

207

Sing a Song of Sixpence

The tune to which these words are sung is an old Scottish song, "Calder Fair." The sixteenth century is usually given as the origin of the words. Their significance, as in many old rhymes, is stretched beyond reason, but, say some, they are merely to indicate a culinary treat which was not uncommon at the time.

Sing A Song Of Six -pence, a pock - et full of rye;

Four and twen -ty black - birds baked in a pie!

When the pie was o - pened, the birds be-gan to sing;

Was-n't that a dain-ty dish to set be-fore a King?

2. The King was in the countinghouse,
   Counting out his money,
   The Queen was in the parlor,
   Eating bread and honey;
   The maid was in the garden,
   Hanging out the clothes;
   When down came a blackbird
   And snipped off her nose.

Skip to My Lou

Children never weary of this American classic.

CHORUS

Lou, Lou, Skip To My Lou; Lou, Lou, Skip To My Lou;

Lou, Lou, Skip To My Lou; Skip To My Lou, my dar - ling.

1. Lost my part - ner, what - 'll I do?

Lost my part - ner, what -'ll I do? Lost my part - ner,

What -'ll I do? Skip To My Lou, my dar - ling.

2. I'll get another one, prettier than you (3 times)
Skip to my lou, my darling.
Chorus:

3. Gone again, skip to my lou (3 times)
Skip to my lou, my darling.
Chorus:

4. Fly's in the buttermilk, shoo, shoo, shoo (3 times)
Skip to my lou, my darling.
Chorus:

5. A little red wagon, painted blue (3 times)
Skip to my lou, my darling.
Chorus:

Sourwood Mountain

Another American square-dance song. It is only a few bars long, but it is wide and deep.

1. Chick-ens a-crow-in' on Sour-Wood Moun-tain,
4. I got a gal at the head of the hol-ler,

Ho-de-ing-dong-dee-dle-al-ley-day. So man-y pret-ty gals
If she won't come, then

Sweet Betsy from Pike

A parody of a hit music-hall song of the 1840s, "Villikins and His Dinah." It became a sort of unofficial anthem of the California emigrants.

1. Oh, don't you re - mem - ber Sweet Bet - sy From Pike, She crossed the big moun - tains with her lov - er Ike, With two yoke of ox - en and one yal - ler dog And an

old Shang - hai roost - er and one spot - ted hog.

CHORUS

Hoo -dle dang dang fol - de - do Hoo -dle dang fol - de-day.

2. They got to the desert where Betsy give out,
Down on the sand she lay rolling about,
Ike he gazed at her with sobs and with sighs,
"Won't you get up, sweet Betsy? You'll get sand in your eyes."
Chorus:

3. Well, the oxen run off and the Shanghai it died,
The last piece of bacon that morning was fried,
Ike got discouraged and Betsy got mad,
And the dog wagged his tail and looked wonderfully sad.
Chorus:

4. Ike and sweet Betsy attended a dance,
Ike wore a pair of his Pike County pants,
Betsy was dressed up in ribbons and rings.
Quoth Ike, "You're an angel, but where are your wings?"
Chorus:

5. A miner come up, says, "Will you dance with me?"
"I will, you old hoss, if you don't make too free;
Tell you the reason, if you want to know why,
Doggone you, I'm chock full of strong alkali."
Chorus:

Taps

Based on an older unofficial bugle call used by the brigade of General Dan Butterfield. The general didn't care for the regulation Taps, and asked his bugler, Norton, to write a new one. He did, and it caught on and gradually spread. These words used to be sung to the call "Put out the lights/Go to sleep/Go to sleep, go to sleep, go to sleep/Put out the lights, go to sleep/Go to sleep."

Day is done, Gone the sun From the lake, From the hill, From the sky; All is well, safe - ly rest; God is nigh.

Ten Little Indians

*Written by Septimus Winner, titled "Ten Little Injuns," about 1860. It was popular in
minstrel shows of the period.*

One lit-tle, two lit-tle, three lit-tle In - dians;
Ten Lit-tle, nine lit-tle, eight lit-tle In - dians;

four lit-tle, five lit-tle, six lit-tle In - dians;
seven lit-tle, six lit-tle, five lit-tle In - dians;

Seven lit-tle, eight lit-tle, nine lit-tle In - dians,
Four lit-tle, three lit-tle, two lit-tle In - dians,

Ten lit-tle In - dian boys.
One lit-tle In - dian boy.

There's a Hole in My Bucket

A lilting, charming song of Pennsylvania Dutch origin.

WILLIE There's a hole in my buck-et, dear Li-za, dear Li-za, There's a
But the straw is too long, dear Li-za, dear Li-za, But the

hole in my buck-et, dear Li-za, a —— hole. LIZA Mend the
straw is too long, dear Li-za, then —— what? LIZA Cut the

hole then, dear Wil-lie, dear Wil-lie, you sil-ly, Mend the
straw then, dear Wil-lie, dear Wil-lie, you sil-ly, Cut the

hole then, dear Wil - lie, you sil -ly, mend ___ it. WILLIE With
straw then, dear Wil - lie, you sil -ly, cut the straw. WILLIE With

what shall I mend it, dear Li - za, dear Li - za, With ___
what shall I cut it, dear Li - za, dear Li - za, With ___

what shall I mend it, dear Li- za, with ___ what? With a
what shall I cut it, dear Li -za, with ___ what? LIZA With a

straw, then, dear Wil -lie, dear Wil-lie, you sil - ly, With a
knife, then, dear Wil -lie, dear Wil-lie, you sil - ly, With a

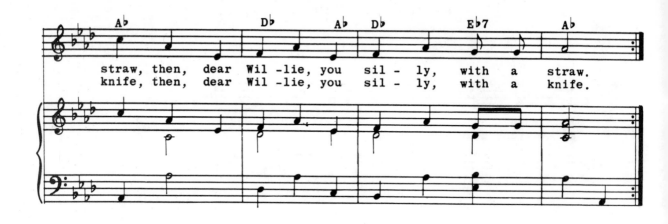

straw, then, dear Wil-lie, you sil - ly, with a straw.
knife, then, dear Wil-lie, you sil - ly, with a knife.

WILLIE: But the knife is too dull, etc.
LIZA: Whet the knife, etc.

WILLIE: With what will I whet it? etc.
LIZA: With a stone, etc.

WILLIE: But the stone is too rough, etc.
LIZA: Smooth the stone, etc.

WILLIE: With what shall I smooth it? etc.
LIZA: With water, etc.

WILLIE: In what shall I carry it? etc.
LIZA: In a bucket, etc.

WILLIE: But there's a hole in my bucket, etc.
LIZA: (spoken) Then mend it, oh, Willie!

There Was an Old Lady

A song in which the things accumulate, not the numbers, such as "The House That Jack Built." Burl Ives popularized it here in 1953, but it was known in England for a half century before.

1. There Was An Old La-dy who swal-lowed a fly, I don't know why she swal-lowed a fly, Per-haps she'll die. 2. There Was An Old La-dy who swal-lowed a spi-der that wrig-gled and wrig-gled and tick-led in-side her; She

swal - lowed the spi - der to catch the fly, But

I don't know why she swal-lowed the fly, Per-haps she'll die.

* Alternate melody after second verse

swal - lowed the spi - der to catch the fly, But

3. There was an old lady who swallowed a bird,
   Now, ain't it absurd to swallow a bird;
   She swallowed the bird to catch the spider,
   She swallowed the spider to catch the fly, etc.

4. There was an old lady who swallowed a cat,
   Now fancy that, to swallow a cat, etc.

5. There was an old lady who swallowed a dog,
   Oh, what a hog to swallow a dog, etc.

6. There was an old lady who swallowed a cow,
   I don't know how she swallowed a cow, etc.

7. There was an old lady who swallowed a horse,
   (Spoken) SHE DIED, OF COURSE!

This Old Man

An English number song, not too well known here until an Ingrid Bergman movie, in which it was sung, made it world famous in 1960–61.

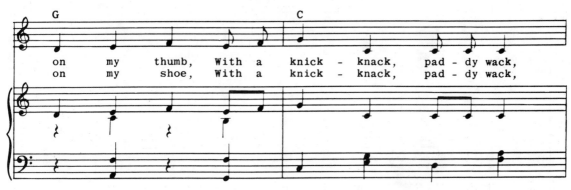

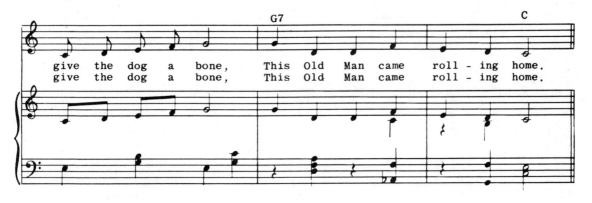

3. This old man, he played three,
   He played knick-knack on my knee, etc.

4. This old man, he played four,
   He played knick-knack on my door, etc.

5. This old man, he played five,
   He played knick-knack on my hive, etc.

6. This old man, he played six,
   He played knick-knack on my sticks, etc.

7. This old man, he played seven,
   He played knick-knack up in heaven, etc.

8. This old man, he played eight,
   He played knick-knack on my gate, etc.

9. This old man, he played nine,
   He played knick-knack on my vine, etc.

10. This old man, he played ten,
    He played knick-knack all over again, etc.

Three Blind Mice

The most famous round in the English language. Although it is over three hundred and fifty years old, it didn't appear in a children's book until the 1840s and 1850s, in **The Nursery Rhymes of England** *by James O. Halliwell.*

Three Blind Mice, Three Blind Mice,

See how they run, See how they run! They

all run af-ter the farm-er's wife; She cut off their tails with a carv-ing knife, Did ev-er you see such a sight in your life as Three Blind Mice.

The Tree in the Wood

Several versions were collected in the Southern Appalachians by Cecil Sharp in 1916–18. It is sometimes known as "The Green Grass (or leaves) Grew All Around."

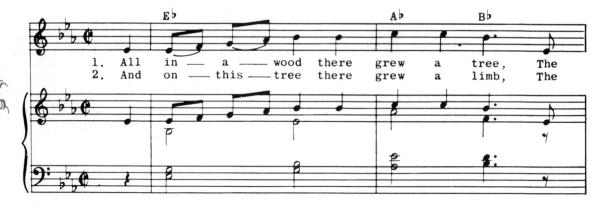

1. All in a wood there grew a tree, The
2. And on this tree there grew a limb, The

fi - nest tree you ev - er did see; The
fi - nest limb you ev - er did see; The

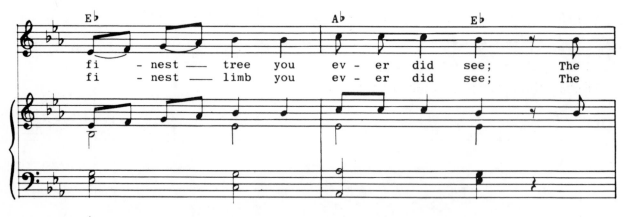

tree was in the wood, (The) And the green leaves grew all a-
limb was on the tree, (The)

round,   a - round,   a-round,   And   the   green   leaves   grew   all   a - round.

3. And on this limb there was a branch, etc.

4. And on this branch there was a nest, etc.

5. And in this nest there was an egg, etc.

6. And in this egg there was a bird, etc.

7. And on this bird there was a wing, etc.

8. And on this wing there was a feather, etc.

*Repeat this measure as often as necessary.

Turkey in the Straw

An early American minstrel song, very popular in Andrew Jackson's time, and sounding, somehow, like Old Hickory himself.

1. As I was a-gwine on down the road, With a
2. Went out to milk and I did-n't know how, I

tired team and a heav-y load, I
milked the goat in-stead of the cow, A

cracked my ___ whip ___ and the lead-er sprung; I ___
mon - key ___ sit-tin' on a pile of straw A -

says day - day ___ to the wag- on tongue.
wink - in' at ___ his ___ moth-er-in - law.

CHORUS

Tur- key In The Straw (Whistle) Tur-key In The Straw,

(Whistle) Roll 'em up and twist 'em up a high tuck- a -haw, And ___

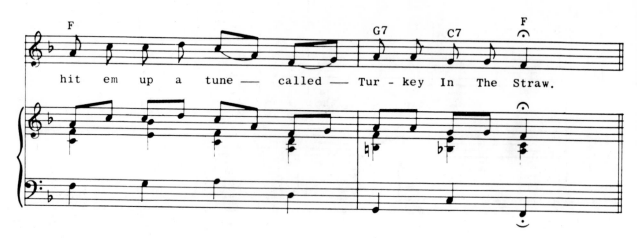

hit em up a tune — called — Tur - key In The Straw.

3. Met Mr. Catfish comin' downstream,
   Says Mr. Catfish, "What does you mean?"
   Caught Mr. Catfish by the snout,
   And turned Mr. Catfish wrong side out.
   Chorus:

4. Came to the river and I couldn't get across,
   Paid five dollars for an old blind hoss,
   Wouldn't go ahead, nor he wouldn't stand still,
   So he went up and down like an old saw mill.
   Chorus:

5. As I came down the new cut road,
   Met Mr. Bullfrog, met Miss Toad,
   And ev'ry time Miss Toad would sing,
   Ole Bullfrog cut a pigeon wing.
   Chorus:

6. Oh, I jumped in the seat, and I gave a little yell,
   The horses run away, broke the wagon all to hell;
   Sugar in the gourd and honey in the horn,
   I never was so happy since the hour I was born.
   Chorus:

The Twelve Days of Christmas

A great "cumulative" song, that is, one in which the verses accumulate as they are sung. It has become so well known in the past fifteen years that we see the song on napkins, Christmas cards, cartoons, etc. The first recording in this country was made by the author of this book in 1945.

1. On the first day of Christ-mas my true love gave to me a part-ridge — in a pear tree. ——— On the sec-ond day of Christ-mas my true love gave to me two tur-tle doves and a part-ridge — in a pear

tree. ____ On the third day of Christ-mas my true love gave to me

three·French — hens, two tur-tle doves and a part- ridge — in a pear

tree. ____ On the fourth day of Christ-mas my true love gave to me

four col-ly birds, three French — hens, two tur-tle doves and a part- ridge —

in a pear tree.— On the fifth day of Christ-mas my true love gave to

me five gold—rings, four—col-ly birds, three French hens, two—tur-tle

doves And a part-ridge—in a pear tree.— On the sixth day of Christ-mas my

Verses 6 - 12

true love gave to me   six geese a-lay-ing,   five gold — rings, four—col-ly birds,

three French hens, two—tur-tle doves And a part-ridge—in a pear tree.

7. Seven swans a-swimming . . .

8. Eight maids a-milking . . .

9. Nine pipers playing . . .

10. Ten ladies dancing . . .

11. Eleven lords a-leaping . . .

12. Twelve fiddlers fiddling . . .

Twinkle, Twinkle, Little Star

The tune is of French or German origin, and was used by Mozart and Dohnanyi. The poem was written by Jane Taylor (with her sister Ann) in a collection of nursery rhymes in 1806.

Twink - le, Twink - le, Lit - tle Star,

How I won - der what you are;

Uncle Reuben

Collected by me in New York about 1939–40, from the singing of Ruth Cleveland.

CHORUS

C   G7   C   (Whispered)   G7

Un -cle Reu-ben caught a 'coon, done gone, Chick- a-chick, done

C (Whispered)   G7   C   (Whispered)   G7

gone, Chick-a-chick, done gone, Chick- a-chick, Un-cle Reu-ben caught a 'coon, done

2. Possum up a 'simmon tree,
   Raccoon on the ground.
   Raccoon say, "Mr. Possum, won't you shake one 'simmon down?"
   Chorus:

3. If you love me, Liza Jane,
   Put your hand in mine.
   You won't lack for no corn bread
   As long as the sun do shine.
   Chorus:

Under the Spreading Chestnut Tree

A modernized English folk song, related to older songs, such as "Go No More A-Rushing," which was used by William Byrd and Giles Farnaby. It undoubtedly seems to be mixed up with an English version of our famous Riddle Song, known there as the Paradox Song. English music-hall singers made it famous in the early twentieth century.

Un-der The Spread - ing Chest - nut Tree,

When I held you on my knee, We were hap - py

as could be, Un-der The Spread- ing Chest - nut Tree.

We Gather Together

Today we sing it as a Thanksgiving hymn, although it was written as a regular Sunday hymn of thanks by a Dutchman (Ankman), at the end of the fifteenth century, to give thanks for the Netherlands' freedom from Spanish domination. The tune is an old Dutch song called "Kremser," and the English words were written by Dr. Theodore Baker.

press - ing cease them from dis - tress - ing, Sing
gin - ning the fight we were ___ win - ning, Thou,

prais - es to His name, He for - gets not His own.
Lord, was at our side, Let the glo - ry be Thine.

3. We all do extol Thee, Thou leader in battle
   And pray that Thou still our Defender wilt be.
   Let Thy congregation escape tribulation;
   Thy name be praised! Thy people be free.

We Three Kings

Written by a New England minister, born in 1820, died in 1891. It is often mistaken, because of its modal tune, as of much older origin.

REFRAIN

O star of won - der, star of night,
Star with roy - al beau - ty bright, West - ward lead - ing,
still pro -ceed - ing, Guide us to thy per - fect light.

Melchior: Born a King on Bethlehem's plain,
Gold I bring, to crown Him again;
King forever, ceasing never,
Over us all to reign.
Refrain:

Caspar: Frankincense to offer have I,
Incense owns a Deity nigh,
Pray'r and praising, all men raising,
Worship Him, God most high.
Refrain:

Balthazar: Myrrh is mine, its bitter perfume,
Breathes a life of gathering gloom,
Sorrowing, sighing, bleeding, dying,
Seal'd in the stone-cold tomb.
Refrain:

All: Glorious now behold Him arise,
King and God and Sacrifice,
Alleluia, alleluia,
Earth to the heav'ns replies.
Refrain:

We Wish You a Merry Christmas

An English street carol which became popular here with the great wave of city interest in folk song in the late 1930s.

1. We Wish You A Mer – ry Christ – mas, We
2. Now bring us some fig – gy pud – ding, Now

Wish You A Mer – ry Christ – mas, We Wish You A Mer – ry
bring us some fig – gy pud – ding, Now bring us some fig – gy

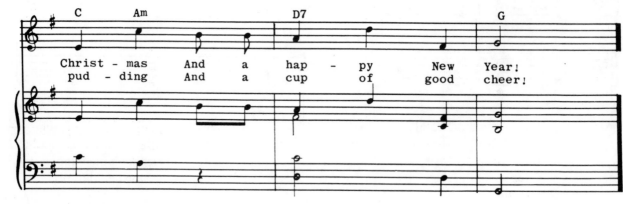

Christ – mas And a hap – py New Year!
pud – ding And a cup of good cheer!

3. We won't go until we get some,
   We won't go until we get some,
   We won't go until we get some,
   So bring it out here.

4. (Repeat first verse.)

When Johnny Comes Marching Home

Attributed to a bandmaster of the Northern Army in the Civil War, Patrick Gilmore.

1. When John-ny Comes March - ing Home a -gain, Hur -
2. Get read - y for —— the Ju - bi - lee, Hur -

rah! —— Hur -rah! —— We'll give him a heart - y
rah! —— Hur -rah! —— We'll give —— the he - ro

wel - come then, Hur - rah! —— Hur - rah! —— The
three times three, Hur - rah! —— Hur - rah! —— The

men will cheer, — the boys will shout, the To
lau - rel wreath — is read - y now

la - dies, they — will all turn out, And we'll
place up - on — his loy - al brow, And we'll

all feel gay When John -ny Comes March - ing Home. ——
all feel gay When John -ny Comes March - ing Home. ——

3. In eighteen hundred and sixty-one, Hurrah! Hurrah!
   That was when the war begun, Hurrah! Hurrah!
   In eighteen hundred and sixty-two, both sides were falling to,
   And we'll all drink stone wine, when Johnny comes marching home.

4. In eighteen hundred and sixty-three, Hurrah! Hurrah!
   Abe Lincoln set the darkies free, Hurrah! Hurrah!
   In eighteen hundred and sixty-three, Old Abe set the darkies free,
   And we'll all drink stone wine, when Johnny comes marching home.

5. In eighteen hundred and sixty-four, Hurrah! Hurrah!
   Abe called for five hundred thousand more, Hurrah! Hurrah!
   In eighteen hundred and sixty-five, they talked rebellion — strife;
   And we'll all drink stone wine, when Johnny comes marching home.

Where Is Thumbkin?

Another finger-play song, which delineates the fingers themselves.

1. Where Is Thumb-kin? Where Is Thumb-kin?
2. Where is point-er? Where is point-er?

Here I am, here I am; How are you to-day, sir?
Here I am, here I am; How are you to-day, sir?

Ver-y well I thank you, Run a-way, run a-way.
Ver-y well I thank you, Run a-way, run a-way.

3. Where is middle? Where is middle?

4. Where is ringer? Where is ringer?

5. Where is pinky? Where is pinky?

Where, Oh Where, Has My Little Dog Gone?

Sung by the Christy minstrels in the late 1800s. It was known variously as "The Dutchman's Wee Dog," "Der Deutscher Dog," etc.

O Where, O Where Has My Lit-tle Dog Gone? O where, O where can he be? ——————— With his ears cut short and his tail cut long, O where, O where can he be? ——————

White Coral Bells

This song might have come from Germany or Holland. There is some evidence of this, though not conclusive.

Oh, don't you wish that you could hear them ring?

That will hap-pen on-ly when the fai - ries sing;

Yankee Doodle

At the time of the French and Indian War, a British Army doctor, Richard Schuckburg, was so amused by the American country-bumpkin troops-to-be who were gathering together near Albany that he wrote this song. Other verses and parodies have been added since.

A   E7

1. Fath - er and I went down to camp a -
2. And there —— was Cap - tain Wash - ing - ton up -

A   E7   A   A7

long with Cap - tain Good - in, and there we saw the
on a slap - pin' stal - lion, and all the men and

men and boys as thick as hast - y pud - din'.
boys a - round, I guess there was a mil - lion.

CHORUS

Yan -kee Doo - dle keep it up, Yan - kee Doo - dle dan - dy,

Mind the mus-ic and the step, and with the girls be han - dy.

3. Yankee Doodle went to town
   Ridin' on a pony,
   Stuck a feather in his cap
   And called it macaroni. .
   Chorus:

Index of First Lines

253

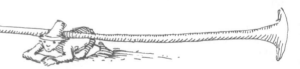